HANDBOOK

FOR THE

AMATEUR LAPIDARY

BY

J. HARRY HOWARD

AUTHOR OF

THE WORKING OF SEMI-PRECIOUS STONES

DESIGNED TO PROVIDE PRACTICAL
INSTRUCTION IN ALL KINDS OF GEM
CUTTING FOR THE BEGINNER AND
FOR THE ADVANCED AMATEUR. : :

Martino Publishing
Mansfield Centre, CT
2012

Martino Publishing
P.O. Box 373,
Mansfield Centre, CT 06250 USA

www.martinopublishing.com

ISBN   978-1-61427-271-7

© *2012 Martino Publishing*

Cover design by T. Matarazzo

Printed in the United States of America On 100% Acid-Free Paper

HANDBOOK

FOR THE

AMATEUR LAPIDARY

BY

J. HARRY HOWARD
AUTHOR OF
THE WORKING OF SEMI-PRECIOUS STONES

DESIGNED TO PROVIDE PRACTICAL
INSTRUCTION IN ALL KINDS OF GEM
CUTTING FOR THE BEGINNER AND
FOR THE ADVANCED AMATEUR. : :

PUBLISHED
BY
J. H. HOWARD
504 CRESCENT AVENUE
GREENVILLE, S. C.

1935

CONTENTS

INTRODUCTION

Man was cutting, carving and polishing gems long before he began to leave written records of his doings. Many Museums have countless examples of the lapidary work done by those artisans (and artists) who wrought from raw minerals, with exceedingly primitive equipment, objects of art that our modern workers would be hard taxed to surpass.

Today, in the Far East, native artisans, with hand or foot driven wheels are producing perfect polishes on difficult gems, showing workmanship of which we amateurs with full complement of modern equipment may well be envious.

Gem cutting is only one of many arts that are old. Ceramics, woodworking, metal working and so forth are old arts. The thing that is peculiar is that these other arts all have their extensive literatures. One may go to any public library and find many volumes on each of these subjects except gem cutting. These volumes are all-revealing, authoritative and detailed. But the subject of gem cutting is shrouded in mystery. No one has written even in generalities on the subject. The Author, several years ago, conducted a search for such literature. He found absolutely nothing. Much later he learned of and borrowed a copy of Oliver Byrnes "Handbook for the Mechanic, Artisan and Engineer" and found in it an exceedingly interesting chapter on gem cutting. But the volume was written about 75 years ago, probably had a very limited circulation, was never reprinted, and not one library in fifty ever heard of it. That is the only volume the Author has ever found that treats even briefly of gem cutting. This excludes of course such texts as "The Gem Cutters Craft" by Leopold Cleremont which have chapters on the technique of cutting but that treat of it so generally that they cannot be used as instructions.

The art for some reason has always been passed down from generation to generation by apprenticeship only. When the Author began the above mentioned investigation he was told "The cutting of gems can be learned only through an apprenticeship." There is no desire here to picture the art as an easy one to learn nor to minimize the skill that is shown by the work of the professional lapidaries, nor to intimate that the professional could, if he would, reveal all his secrets in one brief volume. The desire is, to lift the cloud of mystery that has always surrounded the operation and show that actually there is nothing mysterious in the practices of the profession, but only certain basic rules, which if obeyed, will bring definite results.

It is hoped that the instructions herein given are sufficiently explicit that the beginner in the work will have no especial difficulties. It is hoped also that they are not so tedious but that they will be readable by those who do not propose to cut gems but who are, nevertheless, interested in the operation.

The technique outlined is not exclusively the work of the Author. His original intention was to "give credit where credit was due." And he wishes now to do this in "blanket form." So many of both professionals and amateurs have contributed their thoughts and ideas that it would be impossible to give all their names. And any list of those generous ones would certainly omit some who deserve mention as having been distinctly helpful. So it is desired here and now to thank the many who have helped to make this volume possible.

Certain periodicals and texts have been consulted and made use of and possibly in some cases quoted. Thanks are extended to the Publishers and Authors in all such cases.

It is not to be understood that this text purports to be a record of the methods used in the shops of professional lapidaries. It is only a record of the schemes used by the Author and his friends to accomplish the desired ends. In most cases the methods probably closely parallel the methods used by professionals. In many cases they probably differ. The object of the volume is to make it possible for the amateur lapidary, either the novice or the advanced worker, to produce work such that it will be a genuine pleasure to him. The writing of such a work involves many difficulties and hazards. No matter how a text is written, one reader will yearn for more details while another will be bored by the tedious explicitness. All readers are asked to take this into account when tempted to criticize the work too severely on either of these scores.

We thank especially Mr. Van Amringe for his kind permission to use his article on "The Staining of Agate." Also we thank the publishers of "Rocks and Minerals" and "The Mineralogist" for permission to use wholly or in part, material that has appeared in their pages.

Mr. F. L. Huston of Arthur A. Crafts Co. by his kind cooperation made possible the presentation of the Chapter on Diamond Polishing.

This book goes out with the sincere hope that it may help many people to find much pleasure in the fascinating pastime of gem cutting.

J.H.H.

Greenville, S. C. U.S.A.
September 1935.

CHAPTER I

SAWING

General Discussion

There are in general use two methods of sawing gem stones. One, using a smooth edged metal disc running with its lower edge submerged in a reservoir of Carborundum grains mixed with water or oil is generally called "mud sawing." The other scheme is a diamond saw, consisting of a metal disc with small diamonds imbedded in its edge. A short discussion of the merits of the two schemes is not out of place.

The mud saw has, in general, nothing to commend it except its low cost. The initial investment is very low and there will be no upkeep except an occasional quart of machine oil and an occasional renewing of the Carborundum grains in the reservoir and this initial expenditure will last literally for years. Against this advantage of low cost are several unfavorable factors. It is "messy" to use. It is very slow. It heats the stone, sometimes causing it to crack and often loosening the stone in the cement with which it is anchored to the holder. The slowness of the operation and its tendency to heat the stones makes it impracticable to saw even small stones held by hand and necessitates rigging up the swinging holder for any small job. The cut made by this method is very rough. The smooth discs wear out of true very rapidly and must be trued.

The diamond saw costs more to operate if the user places no value on his time. But if the user's time is valued at even a nominal amount the diamond saw with its higher speed of cutting is cheaper to operate than the mud saw. It cuts from 5 to 10 times as fast. The job is comparatively clean. Kerosene oil is used as a lubricant and this is easy to wipe off the machine and the workbench. It does not heat the stone excessively. The mud saw heats because grains of Carborundum get on the sides of the disc and continue throughout the cut to grind against the sides of the cut, constantly widening it. In the diamond saw all the abrasive is embedded in the edge of the disc. This, in addition to a minimum of heating, makes for a smoother cut. The stone not being appreciably heated and each cut being done quickly, it is entirely practicable to hold the stone in the hands while doing cuts of considerable size. This means that when one has only a single or even several cuts to make, they may be done without rigging up the swinging holder. The disc being studded on its edge with small diamonds does not wear out of true until and unless some of the diamonds become dislodged from their seats. When this begins to happen to a diamond saw its life is about at an end. Contrary to the case of the plodding mud saw, the diamond saw has a limited life. The length of this life cannot be predicted. It depends on the care with which it is made and the skill with which it is used. Also a tremendous element of chance enters into its life expectancy. No matter how well it is made nor with what care it is used there is always the possibility of an accident. A single flake or sliver of stone may become wedged in the cut in such a way as to strip the diamonds from the disc or a single diamond may come loose and wedge in the cut in such a manner as to quickly ruin the saw.

Sawing with a mud saw seems to give the amateur more trouble than any other operation. It is quite critical as to consistency of mix. Considerable care is required to maintain the right consistency, due to the tendency of the Carborundum grains to be slung by centrifugal force to the bottom and sides of the reservoir. The mix must be frequently agitated. I used the mud saw for several years but was never able to get consistent satisfactory results. In using the diamond saw the beginner will get perfect results but must learn from experience how to protect his saw against injury.

MUD SAWING

This sawing is done with a sheet iron disc about 20 to 22 ga. about 10" in diameter. It should run at a speed of 400 to 500 rpm with its lower edge submerged about 1/2" in a reservoir of thin paste made of No. 100 carbo grains and light machine oil. The stone rides against the disc, being held firmly by the weight of the hinged holder or by a hand against this holder or by weights or springs on the holder. For this assembly see Fig. 1. There is room for much latitude in designing this holder. The one pictured in Fig. 1 is the kind I use and find very satisfactory. It is of utmost simplicity and minimum cost. It consists of a wood block 1" x 12" x 24" hinged to the bench at its lower end. The original hinge pins are removed and long removable pins substituted. When the device is not in use, the pins are drawn and the board is removed from the bench. The block has a narrow slot cut in it at the point where it makes contact with the saw. This slot is just wide enough to take the bodies of heavy round head wood screws which pass through this slot and hold in place a smaller wood block, about 1"x3"x6". The screws are to be loosened and the small block moved endways for the spacing of the cuts on slabs or strips or blocks.

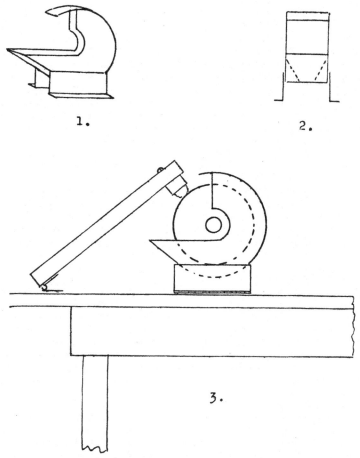

Figure 1.—RIG FOR MUD SAWING.
1. Splash pan—side view.
2. Splash pan—front view showing baffle plates.
3. Assembly.

The stone is to be cemented to the small wood block. After a small block has been used once and is covered with oil, it is to be discarded.

Use chasers cement for anchoring the stone to the block. Melt the cement in a seamless vessel over a slow fire. While it is melting, let the stone and the wood block be warming over another fire. Let the stone be warm enough to be uncomfortable to hold in the hand. Pour some of the cement on the wood block. Set the stone in the cement in proper position and hold it there until the cement is cool enough to sustain the stone in the correct position. Then pour some of the cement in a bank around the base of the stone. If this job is done carefully, the stone will not break loose, though excessive heat may warm the cement enough to allow the stone to move or actually to come loose. When the cement is hard, fasten the block with the wood screws to the hinged arm.

Place under the disc a reservoir similar to that shown in Fig. 1. There must be some kind of guard provided over the front of this reservoir to deflect spatter back into the reservoir. This should be made of sheet tin, cut with snips, bent to shape and readily removable. Fill this reservoir with paste about the consistency of ordinary cream to where the lower edge of disc is submerged about 1/2″. This paste is made, as noted above, of No. 100 carbo powder and a light grade of machine or engine oil.

The troubles that will be encountered have generally been mentioned above but will be suggested again here. The throwing of paste must be controlled by shields made to suit each condition. They should guide the thrown paste back into the reservoir or into a large shallow pan placed under the reservoir. Sheet tin or zinc is obtainable everywhere, costs little and is easy to work. Often a cloth apron will be found effective where it is found difficult to properly control the paste with the metal shield alone.

Keeping the paste at right consistency is not an easy job and must be learned by experience. It must be stirred frequently to keep the carbo grains in suspension, and either oil or carbo must be added occasionally as the mix appears too thick or too thin. Its thickness will of course vary greatly with its temperature, and this should be taken into consideration when beginning work with the oil cold.

The discs will quickly develop flats and begin pounding. Some of this may be tolerated but not too much of it. When the saw is pounding, cutting is very slow, the cement may be cracked and loosen the stone or the stone itself may be broken. There is no remedy except to change discs. The user should see to it that the discs are true when put in service. I prefer to have 1/2 dozen or more of these discs and to use them successively until all or nearly all are out of true, then take them to a machine shop for retruing. The job can, however, be done at home with a cutting tool supported on the tool rest of the grinding head.

Alternate Method.—This has some merits. The spatter is not so hard to clean up. It does not heat the stone so fast (due to lower speed), but the cutting rate is much lower than with the oil mix. Flats do not develop so fast, due to the lower machine speed. The wood blocks and cement may be used over and over as there is no oil on them.

This alternate scheme differs from the one outlined above only in the fact that the paste is made of water or turpentine with some clay flour added, and the speed is reduced to from 100 to 300 rpm.

If water is used for mixing, it is likely to whip up into a froth through the trapping of countless small pockets of air, and this slows up the work tremendously. If turpentine is used, it will not froth, but turpentine evaporates quite rapidly and the mix thickens rapidly through this loss. Also, I have never been sure that turpentine is absolutely safe for this work. It is very inflammable, and while I have never had it to happen, I have always felt there was some danger of its being ignited from a spark thrown from the work.

The exact amount of clay flour to be used is not critical. The purpose of the clay flour is to add stickiness to the mix. A good handful in the mix, say about 1/2 as much flour as carbo, is sufficient. The clay must be clean and free from grit. It is best to buy this material screened rather than to try to use "home made" clay. The sawing depends on the maintenance of actual contact between the stone and the edge of the disc with its adhering carbo grains. If the clay has in it grains of sand larger than the carbo grains, these grains of sand will adhere to the edge of the disc, and during the time required for the grain to roll across the cut there will be no abrasive action from the carbo.

General Notes on Mud Sawing.—In cementing stones onto blocks do not allow the cement to get too hot or it may ignite. Also if heated too much some of its more volatile components will be lost. But the cement must be wholly melted.

The tendency of the discs to develop flats is somewhat in proportion to their speed. The rate at which flats develop also depends on the size of the stone being sawed. The wider the face of the stone, the longer may be the flat that may be present without giving trouble.

The pressure must be constant and the stone must not be allowed to "bounce" on the wheel, as this tends to start flats.

All other factors being constant, the rate of cutting is about in proportion to the speed of the saw. It is for this reason that the oil mix is about twice as fast as the water mix. The cutting rate in agate of medium hardness should be about 3 sq. in. per hour with the oil mix.

A persistent "swishing" sound indicates proper cutting.

The pressure put on the stone has some effect on the rate of cutting but does not seem to be tremendously important. I believe that in general the greater the pressure, the faster the cutting, but that the difference in rate is not at all in direct proportion to the pressure. Positively, the pressure should not be great enough to slow down the disc.

One very real disadvantage of the mud method of sawing is that it takes much more power than an amateur uses in any other operation. This is because of the wedging of carbo grains between the disc and the sides of the cut. These act as brakes. A 1/4 H.P. motor is sufficient for any other operation, but if mud sawing is to be done for long periods it may seriously overload a 1/4 H.P. motor.

One precaution that is very important in mud sawing is to do everything possible to guard the bearings of the grinding head against the carbo mix getting into them. Most grinders are made with the wheel flange butting against the bearing. Under this condition it is almost impossible to prevent trouble. The manufacturers of grinding heads will build special, for the payment of a small extra, a machine with extended shaft with the wheel flange as far away from the bearing as the buyer may specify. With these machines a cloth or metal hood may be placed over the bearing to protect it. In the absence of this special feature the conventional machine must have its bearings guarded as well as possible.

Be sure that the sawing discs are drilled to fit snugly on the arbor. In buying a grinding head be sure that the arbor nut threads do not extend entirely back to the wheel flange, as in that case you could not put thin discs on the arbor and have them true. The disc would drop down into a thread and be thrown out of true.

In making or buying the reservoirs do not omit the two oblique baffle plates. They are for the purpose of keeping the carbo grains concentrated close to the disc. If these are omitted, the heavy grains will be thrown by centrifugal force into the corners of the reservoir and make much harder the job of keeping the mix at proper consistency.

The "rockholder" described herein is an extremely simple form of this device. They may be and are made in all sorts of designs, including very elaborate and costly affairs. They can all be made sufficiently effective, though certainly more convenient ones may be designed than the one described herein. As a matter of fact, while I began work with just such a one as is pictured, I have since replaced it with one made of steel flats and angles, but the design is the same.

The arbor should fit snugly in its bearings, and the entire outfit should be as free as possible from vibration. Excessive vibration is a fruitful source of trouble. It may be caused by too frail work bench, loose bearings, obround disc, etc. Whatever the cause, it must be remedied before satisfactory sawing can be done.

Morse in "Notes on Steel Disc Sawing" says, "The stone should be riding against the disc when the machine is started and should stay against it until the saw has stopped turning." He also notes that the wheel flanges should be large enough to hold the saw in its true plane and that the belt should be smooth and tight

Never start a cut on a sharp edge, as doing so may start a flat.

When stones are held in cement for sawing, the cement gets into irregularities of the stone and is hard to get out. Soak the cut pieces in gasoline, and all oil, carbo grains and cement may be washed off together.

The Norton Company has recently put on the market a Boron Carbide under the trade name "Norbide." It is claimed that this material is very superior in hardness to any other material than the diamond. Those who have used it in the mud saw are very enthusiastic about its behavior. By adding an occasional tablespoonful of Norbide to the mix the sawing is speeded considerably.

THE DIAMOND SAW

General Discussion

The diamond saw is the amateur's best friend. It works from five to ten times as fast as the mud saw; it makes a smoother cut; it has less objectionable spatter and is much easier to put into and out of service on a grinder that is also used for other work. While it is not, so far, as generally used by amateurs as the mud saw, it is becoming more popular as its merits become better known. It is almost universally used by professional lapidaries. There are several reasons for the slowness of its adoption by amateurs. It was not and is generally still not deemed practicable for a manufacturer to standardize and manufacture and distribute this saw as a uniform product. So they were not advertised. There was for a long time no reliable information made public as to how to make and use them. It is rather difficult to properly break and size bortz for use in these saws, and diamond dealers did not advertise the diamond crushed and sized. Some diamond dust that has been offered for sale was very variable in quality, often carrying many impurities. The proper metal for making discs was not readily obtainable in small quantities. The grinding heads used by many amateurs were of such poor quality that they would not give satisfactory results with a diamond saw. The cost of making or of buying the saws has seemed too high for the average amateur.

Most of these conditions have been remedied. It is still probably not best for a manufacturer to make and sell these. The ratio of cost of labor to cost of material is rather high. If a manufacturer furnishes this labor, he must have a profit on it, and this makes the cost of the saw more than many users feel they can afford to pay. Again, the manufacturer has no control over the kind of machine on which the saw is to be used. Nor over the technique of the user. As these factors are tremendously important in the success or failure of the operation, and as they are so often unfavorable, the life of such saws is very doubtful and the percentage of dissatisfied users is very high. Amateurs are coming to realize more and more that their most important piece of equipment is the grinding head and are using better ones. The saws can be made successfully by the user, and the cost, when this is done, is not excessive. The average user may destroy several saws before he learns how to protect them against injury, but when this lesson has been learned, the user's sawing troubles are at an end.

Making the Saw—Use Spring Brush Copper or Phosphor Bronze for the disc. The amateur will probably not want a saw larger than 10″. For this and all smaller sizes use 22 ga. metal. Bore the disc a neat fit for the spindle and turn it to perfectly round. Place the disc on the spindle with flanges on both sides and tighten in place. With a thin bladed knife and a light hammer, make a series of cuts straight across the edge of the disc, 1/25″ (1 mm.) apart and the same depth. The disc is now ready to be charged. There are several ways to do this, differing in detail only. The essential is to get grains of diamonds distributed fairly evenly over all the edge of the disc and driven into the slots.

For the purpose of this description assume that 1/4 carat of dust will be used for a 6″ saw or 1/2 carat of dust for a 10″ saw. See later note for further details as to quantity to be used. Mix the diamond dust with olive oil or castor oil to make a thin paste. Apply most of this to the edge of the disc, saving back a small amount to be used later in the operation. This distributing may be done in either of several ways. Small lots of the paste may be picked up with a matchstick or a tooth pick and "smeared" along the edge of the disc. Or the mix may be spread on a hard flat metal surface about 1" x 3" or 4" and the disc rolled repeatedly, with considerable pressure through this area. Or the mix may be spread on a steel roller held in a support such as a wheel dresser handle. The roller is then pressed solidly against the disc as the disc is revolved slowly, the roller handle being supported on the tool rest. Or small lots of the paste may be picked up on a finger and rubbed along the edge of the disc. When the paste is nearly all distributed, take a light hammer and proceed to drive the grains into the edge of the disc with light blows. Nearly all the grains will enter nicks, which is as it should be. Some of the grains will escape the driving and adhere to the sides of the disc. These are to be pushed back with the fingers to the edge of the disc and pounded into place. This is to be repeated until no loose grains are present.

Next a large flat stone such as agate or quartz, any fairly hard stone, is anchored in the swinging rock holder. The belt should be taken off the grinder so that the shaft turns freely. The stone is lowered gently against the disc. Now rock the disc back and forth with short strokes of 2" to 4" while the stone is pressed firmly against it. The purpose of this is to wear the metal down where it is too high and to drag the metal more firmly around the grains of diamond and to tear loose any partially imbedded grains that might later come loose and wreck the saw if it were running at high speed. When the rocking has been in progress several minutes, stop and examine. Where bright spots appear, apply a little of the dust that was saved for this purpose, hammer it into place and proceed with the rocking. Any time spent in this operation is well spent. It must not be slighted. It may require as much as 45 minutes though 15 to 20 minutes is more nearly the average. The job is finished when no bright spots show on the edge of the disc but the entire edge is a dull whitish color from the rock dust.

Using the Saw.—The saw must fit snugly on its spindle and must be perfectly round. It is best that it not have any "wobble," though, with the hard rolled thin discs we use, it is almost impossible to attain perfection in this respect. To stiffen the saw and to avoid as much wobble as possible it is well to install flanges on both sides of the saw, these flanges extending as nearly to the edge as will permit the saw to reach through the material that is to be cut.

The same stone holding device that was described for use with mud saws is suitable here. If several large slabs are to be cut, it will pay to cement the stone onto the wood black as before

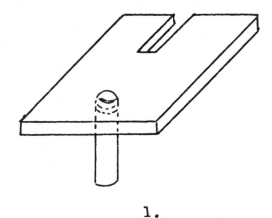

1.

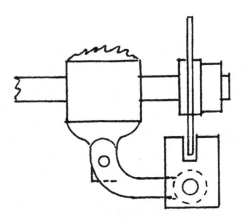

2.

Figure 2.—PLATFORM.
        For supporting stones for diamond sawing.
        1. Detail of platform.
        2. Assembly.

described.   However, if only medium sized cuts are to be made, it is easier to hold the stone by hand on the swinging holder, because the sawing is fast and there is little heating.   It is well, if stone is to be held by hand, to screw or tack a small strip of wood along the lower edge of the block, forming a ledge for the stone to bear against.   This ledge to have a slot sawed in it at the point where otherwise it would touch the disc.   If only a few small cuts are to be made, it may not be necessary or desirable to rig up the swinging holder.   Such cases may be readily taken care of with a small platform anchored to the tool rest holder with which your grinding head is equipped.   See Fig. 2. The stone may be held free in the hands on top of this platform and pressed against the saw, though a wood cradle such as is shown in Fig. 3 is safer.   There is danger when holding a stone

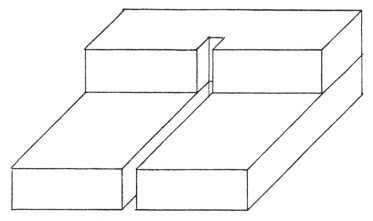

Figure 3.—WOOD CRADLE.
      For supporting small stones for sawing with diamond saw.
      Rests on platforms shown in Fig. 2.

by hand that it may bind the saw and be jerked out of position and injure the saw.

The next job is to provide a means of applying a lubricant to the work.   This lubricant may be applied either by a drip system from an overhead reservoir or by direct application from beneath the saw (letting the edge of the saw actually run in a bath of the lubricant) or by indirect application from beneath the saw through some such medium as a sponge.   I prefer the latter method and will describe it.   Provide first a large shallow pan to place beneath the whole saw and reservoir assembly to catch

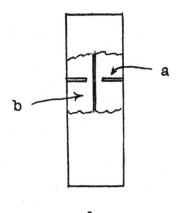

1.

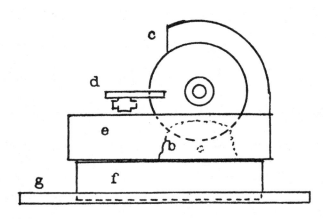

2.

Figure 4.—SPLASH PAN ASSEMBLY FOR DIAMOND
        SAWING.
    1. Plan of splash pan with sponge.
    2. Assembly.
        a. Pins soldered in pan.
        b. Sponge split in center.
        c. Cloth apron on front of guard.
        d. Platform for supporting stones.
        e. Reservoir.
        f. Wood block.
        g. Shallow large pan.

the most of the inevitable spatter. This pan is not fastened to either the work bench or the reservoir. The reservoir, see Fig. 4, is a long narrow pan about 4″ wide x 4″ deep x 12″ to 18″ long, with a spatter shield fastened to its rear end and projecting over and down somewhat in front of the saw to a point where it will just miss interfering with the feeding of the stone to the saw. Cloth aprons may be hung on the front and on both sides of the saw, and if this is done very little spatter will escape the large flat pan. At a point directly under where the saw will be located, solder two sharp pins to the sides of the small pan, on the inside, pointing toward each other and with their points about 1 1/2″ apart. These are to hold a sponge in position. Choose a sponge somewhat greater in diameter than the width of the small pan and rather regular in outline. Split this sponge in the center to form a slot in which the saw will revolve. Compress the sponge, slip it down between the two pin points, and force the two halves onto the pins so that the sponge will be held in place with its cut faces bearing against each other. Now, slip this assembly under the saw, raise it up, with the saw in the slot in the sponge, until the saw is about an inch from the bottom of the pan. Put wood blocks under the pan to hold it in this position.

Pour kerosene over the sponges on both sides of the saw to wet them thoroughly. Pour about 1/2″ of kerosene in the pan.

The operation is not critical to speed. Definitely, the speed should not be great enough to cause heating, as heat will certainly cause the saw to warp. Somewhere between 400 and 800 rpm for the 10″ size and twice these speeds for the 6″ size will be right, though probably not over 1200 rpm should be a maximum.

The stone having been cemented to the holder (I recommend that a beginner's first cuts be made with the stone cemented to the block regardless of the size of cut) the machine is started. When the saw is up to full speed, bring a flat surface of the stone down gently against the saw. Use light pressure while the cut is being started, increasing it when the cut is under way, and again diminishing it as the cut nears completion. The pressure is not to be great at any time. Remember how the saw is made and that its teeth are small and only held in place by thin fins of soft copper. Don't try to put too much strain on them.

General Notes.—The life of the diamond saw cannot be predicted. It depends on too many factors. Among these are: the care and knowledge that go into its making, the skill with which it is used, and the amount of diamond that is embedded in it. Some users expect from 50 to 150 sq. in. of cut from a charge of 1/4 carat of dust. Others expect 1000 sq. in. and more of cut from a charge of 1 carat of dust. It appears that the life of the saw is definitely greatly affected by the amount of diamond embedded in it (all other factors being equal) and that the length of life is more than in direct proportion to the increased amount of the charge, at least up to a certain point. I think it best to state here limits only and let the individual user arrive by experiment at his own conclusions as to the economical amount of charge. The minimum amount ever recommended for a 10″ saw is 1/4 carat, and for a 6″ saw is 1/8 carat. The maximum amounts recommended for a 10″ saw is one carat and for a 6″ saw is 1/2 carat. I personally do not think the lower limits given above should ever be used. I prefer the upper limit but can recommend 1/2 carat for the 10″ saw and 1/4 carat for the 6″ saw as being satisfactory. Also I suggest that the beginner use no more than these amounts on his first efforts, as he is quite likely to spoil some of his first saws without giving them a chance to serve their normal life.

There is considerable room for variation in the thickness of metal used for the discs. Twenty four ga. is very satisfactory for the 6″ saw but is rather light for the 10″ saw. I prefer 22 ga. for the 10″ saw. The advantage of thicker metal is that they are more likely to be flat. The disadvantage of the thicker metal is that it makes a thicker cut and therefore diamond is being wasted in cutting away superflous material. It is apparent that if we put a given amount of dust in the edge of a disc of a given thickness, it will be twice as concentrated as if it were distributed over the edge of a disc twice as thick.

There is no unanimity of opinion as to correct procedure when a saw needs recharging. Some users insist that when a disc needs a recharge it should be applied on top of the old one, thereby making continued use of whatever diamond is still in the old disc. I have not found this profitable in my own work. I think that usually when a saw becomes dull, it will most likely be also somewhat out of true, and also most of the "set" will be worn away, and when this condition exists I believe it is best to trim off the old edge, retrue the disc and start anew. In pounding or rolling the charge into place a considerable set is given the saw, and this is an important factor in keeping the saw cool as well as in providing a pathway for the blade wide enough to protect the diamond grains against being dragged from their seats.

Many users do their own crushing of grains. I have not found this profitable, though if one feels inclined to try it, it is entirely practicable. Use bortz, which is cheaper and just as good for this purpose as carbon. Lay the piece of bortz on a hard steel block. Cover it thoroughly with olive oil or castor oil. Proceed to break it to sizes wanted, using a machinist's hammer and light blows. The trouble with this scheme is that some of the pieces will be broken too small and therefore wasted while some will be left too large. The ones that are too small will be merely useless, the ones that are too large are worse than useless, as they are quite likely to be torn out of the saw and in coming loose to scrape other grains from their seats. I think it pays to buy diamond already crushed and screened to a reasonable range of sizes. The dust I use runs about 800 pieces per carat.

There are certain precautions to be taken in using the diamond saw, and the observing of these will pay good dividends. The saw must never be started on a sharp edge of material. The safest place to enter it on a new cut is on a flat smooth surface. If there is no flat surface, use a rounded one with as large radius as possible. If the stone has no available smooth surface for beginning the cut, it is best to grind one on it with a carbo wheel.

It is not safe to saw stones with cracks in them. Nor hollow geodes. While this is often necessary, it is only fair to point out that it is very dangerous. A single particle or sliver of rock breaking loose at a crack may become wedged in the cut in such a way as to scrape off the charge from the saw.

Never let a stone or anything else fall against the edge of the saw.

When making the saw be sure to scratch an arrow on the side of it to indicate the direction in which it is to always run.

If a saw loses its charge while making a cut, it is best to abandon that cut and begin a new one far enough from the old that there is no danger of the new breaking into the old. Never try to put a new saw into a cut made by an old saw. Perhaps the saw is not large enough to cut through a given specimen and it is desired to turn the work over and saw from the other side. It is all right to use this expedient but stop the second cut before it quite meets the first one and do the final severing by breaking.

The diamond saw is a precision tool and must be treated as such if it is to give the service you have a right to expect of it.

The supply of lubricant should at all times be liberal. As the kerosene level lowers, renew the supply. Watch it and do not wait for "mud" to begin to collect on the top edge of the cut to indicate that the oil is too low. The embedded diamonds, being about 1000 times as hard as quartz, are not going to wear appreciably. So the saw is going to remain in a constant condition until diamonds come out of it. They can get out only through violent pull or through the copper wearing away from them.   As the diamonds cut a clear path for the disc, there will be no wear on the copper except such as is caused by the cut away material.   This material should be washed out of the cut as quickly as possible to minimize the wear on the copper.   We therefore see that what we have referred to and thought of purely as a lubricant also performs the equally important function of washing away the debris.   It is safest for the beginner to fill his reservoir to where the edge of the disc actually touches the kerosene.

Some users add about 25 percent of machine oil to the kerosene.   This makes the operation more "messy" but may pay on a large job.

The Carborundum Saw

This device deserves mention though I have not found it practicable for general use.

Both the Carborundum Co. and Norton Co. make "Carborundum" saws.   These consist of an abrasive with a shellac binder which gives it some but not much flexibility.   These are highly effective on some materials, but on gem materials they are not entirely satisfactory.   However, they do have a distinct place in this work.   If an amateur is using mud saws only for his sawing and it is desired to do only one or a few small cuts and the amount of such cutting does not justify rigging up the mud saw, the Carborundum Saw is a great convenience.   Use a No. 60 C saw either 1/8" or 1/16" thick by about 6" diameter. Such saws cost very little, and in case one is broken, as often happens, the loss is not serious.

The saw must be plentifully supplied with water.   The material should be fed to the saw by hand.   A rigid rest is not necessary for small cuts and the scheme is not suitable for large cuts.

If the stone is fed to the saw with a fixed straight motion, the saw will take a glaze which will practically stop the cutting. This can be prevented by feeding by hand and with a rocking motion so that a constantly new surface and short arc of contact is presented to the saw.   The speed should be about 5000 sfpm. The exact recommended maximum speed is given by the maker with each saw.   The saw will behave all right when the work is fed by hand unless the cut is deep.   If the cut is deep, the saw will be likely to bind, due to work not being held exactly true.   When this binding occurs, it may snatch the stone from the worker's hand and may also break the saw.   It is well not to stand in line with the saw, as it may throw pieces of itself if it breaks. The rate of wear is high, it develops flats quickly and must be trued often. In short, it is only an emergency proposition.

Wire Sawing

Pierced material can have its holes enlarged or cut to irregular shapes with a wire saw. Irregular or curved sawing may also be done in this way.

If the problem is sawing to irregular lines, such as is often required in mosaics, etc., it had best be done with a solid wire charged with diamond dust. Use either copper or soft iron wire. Stretch it in either a hasksaw frame or a coping saw frame. Stretch it taut. Then "hammer" it with the blade of a heavy knife held at right angles to the wire. (Or hold the knife against the wire and drive it into the wire with light blows of a hammer). Cover the cutting "side" and the adjacent sides of the wire with a series of nicks. Then daub the wire with fairly fine diamond dust mixed with oil. (The grade known as "No. 1" is good). Lay the taut wire on any flat metal surface and drive the diamond into the wire with light blows of a hammer.

Then proceed to saw with it, using it just as you would a coping saw. It will need frequent recharging, but the amount of diamond embedded in each charge is very small. In using it keep it wet with kerosene. The heat developed will be considerable.

If one has only a minor job of this kind to do, it may be very satisfactorily done with Carborundum grains. It is best, if carbo grains are used, to employ a stranded wire of copper or bronze or phosphor bronze, such strand as is used for radio antennae. The carbo grains should be about No. FF mixed with water and daubed frequently on the stranded wire.

This is not a fast cutting operation but is valuable for the occasional job or for smoothing the edges of holes drilled with diamond or tube drills.

CHAPTER II

CABOCHON CUTTING

General Discussion

The cabochon cut (knob shaped) is used on most of the opaque and translucent stones. Also on some that are transparent if they happen to have an especially attractive color but are too badly flawed to cut with facets. Because this type of gem is subject to such wide variation in shape and size, large collections may be built exclusively of it without danger of monotony.

The cutting and polishing routine given here will be based on the most common form of this gem, the form having curved front and flat back. The work to be done in converting a rough stone into a cabochon cut gem will be divided into several headings in their proper sequence. The beginner should not attempt any too radical departures from the routine laid down. There are many ways in which most of the operations can be successfully done. But it makes for a clearer narrative to postpone any discussion of alternate methods to a later time. It is, then, to be understood that the detail here given is not a record of *necessary* steps but is one series that has proven satisfactory and is safe for the beginner to follow.

The equipment and supplies needed for this operation, and which are described more fully in the chapter on Equipment, are:

1   Grinding Head
1   Motor
1   No. 100 Carborundum Wheel
1   No. FF Carborundum Wheel
1   Cast Iron Lap
1   Wood Lap with periphery turned true
2   1" x 6" Hard Felt Wheels
   No. FF Carborundum Powder
   Powdered Pumice Stone
   Tin Oxide
   Oil Cloth Apron
   Chasers Cement
   Lap Sticks
   Splash Pans
   Reservoir
   Sponges for Water Feed
   One-inch Paint Brushes
1   7 to 10 Power Magnifying Glass

It is assumed that stones of from 7 to 5 in hardness will be cut first. This range embraces the more commonly used gems such as opal, obsidian, agate, jasper, malachite, etc. It is suggested that the first few stones cut be about 1/2" wide x 3/4" long x 1/4" thick. Smaller stones would have less work on them but would be harder to hold and would more plainly show irregularities that may exist on one's initial efforts.

The rough material is first to be sawed by methods given in a previous chapter, to approximately the size wanted in the finished gem.

Cutting and Polishing

1. *Rig for Cutting.*—Put the No. 100 Carbo wheel on the grinding head. Belt for a speed of about 5000 sfpm. Or about 1500 rpm for a 10" wheel. The manufacturers of the wheel give, on the label of each wheel, the maximum speed at which the wheel should run, and this instruction should be rigidly obeyed.

Set a splash pan beneath the wheel. This pan may be any one of various designs. The one shown in Figure 5 is suggested

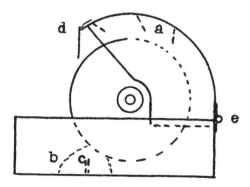

Figure 5.—RESERVOIR FOR CARBO WHEEL GRINDING.
    a. Fins to deflect spatter.
    b. Sponge.
    c. Pin to hold sponge in place.
    d. Cloth apron.
    e. Hinge by which top part may be swung back out of the way when changing wheels.

as simple and effective. It may be made at home, though it is best to have it made at a tin shop of heavy galvanized metal. When the pan is made, have it fitted with some device to hold the sponge in place. This may be done by soldering two sharp pins on the sides of the pan, on the inside, with their points opposite each other and about 1 1/2″ apart. They should be about 1″ from the bottom of the pan and about half way from the front to the rear of the pan.

A sponge is then compressed and slipped between the pin points and forced onto the pins. The sponge is to be of such size and in such position that it will be largely submerged in the water that will be poured over it and its top side will bear gently against the lower edge of the wheel. Block the pan up beneath the wheel with wood blocks until the lower edge of the wheel rests firmly but gently against the sponge. Fill the pan with water to within 1/2″ of the wheel. A cloth apron may be placed over the guard, to hang down just to the wheel in front and well down on both sides of the wheel to minimize the throwing of water. The user should wear a full length waterproof apron. The outfit must be placed where the throwing of water will do no harm, as it is not practicable to entirely prevent it.

2. *Outlining.*—If what is to be the base of the stone is not fairly flat, it should be ground to as nearly flat as can be gotten on this wheel. Then, holding the stone between the thumbs and forefingers of both hands, proceed to grind it to where the base has the correct outline for the finished stone. Let the sides slope slightly toward the peak of the crown. Grind away from the base and toward the peak of the crown. When the correct outline has been gotten, grind a small "working bevel" all around the base. This is to prevent chipping of what would otherwise be a sharp edge. If the stone is especially fragile, it may pay to keep a small bevel ground ahead of the side cutting from the beginning.

Now remove all this present rigging.

3. *Flatting the Base.*—Put on the cast iron lap. Set under it a combined pan and guard such as is shown in Fig. 6. A small amount of No. FF carbo grains made into a paste with water is kept in the pan and applied to the side of the lap with a small paint brush. Change the speed to 800 rpm. Holding the stone by hand, proceed to grind it on the flat side of the lap with the paste applied frequently until the base is positively flat.

Wash the stone and wash the lap. Put on a new pan and guard; use a paste of No. 600 carbo and further smooth the base with this finer paste.

Remove the iron lap and the pan of No. 600 paste. No need of washing the stone this time as the operation is going back to a coarser paste which will give a finer finish because it is used on a softer lap. Change the speed to 400 rpm. Put on a maple

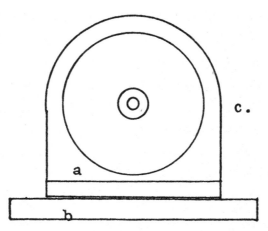

Figure 6.—PAN AND GUARD FOR GRINDING ON SIDE OF
WHEELS.
Pan (a) fastened to wood block (b). Guard (c) integral
with pan.

lap about 2″ thick x 8″ diameter turned true.   Set under it the
pan of No. FF paste.   Smooth the base on the periphery of the
wood lap, still holding the stone by hand.   Apply the paste
freely and often.   Keep the stone moving and change its position in the hands frequently.   When the base is uniformly

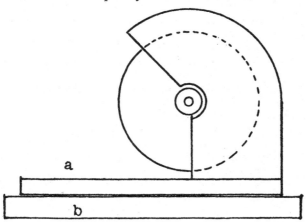

Figure 7.—SPLASH PAN FOR FELT WHEELS.
a.   Shallow pan fastened to wood block (b).

smooth and no scratches made by the carbo are visible under the magnifying glass, the step is finished. The best form of pan for this is shown in Fig. 7.

4. *Polishing the Base.*—Remove the present rig. Wash the stone and wash the hands. Put on a hard felt lap 1" x 6" and place under it a splash pan such as shown in Fig. 7. Mix a batch of pumice powder (or tripoli) with water, into a paste in the pan. Apply to the felt wheel with a paint brush. Still holding the stone by hand proceed to polish the base. Use heavy pressure. Speed 400 rpm. Continue this polishing until, when looked at with the magnifier, the surface is uniformly smooth, free from scratches and dull places, and apparently completely polished. It is now ready for the real polish.

Wash the stone and the hands. Remove the felt lap and the pan and replace with similar lap and similar pan but with paste of tin oxide and water. Speed 800 rpm. Pressure moderate, depending largely on the hardness of the stone. Apply paste frequently, about each 10 seconds. In this operation it is very easy to overheat a stone at the place it happens to be in contact with the wheel, causing it to flake.

The completion of the final polish must be judged by the eye of the worker. A good way to judge it is to wipe the surface clean and dry and hold it so as to catch on it a reflection of some light object such as the electric light or a window. Judge the polish by the sharpness of the outline.

5. *Cementing.*—Provide a lapstick about 4" long, with one end approximately the shape of the outline of the base of the stone but about 1/8" smaller in each dimension. This stick may be whittled from any kind of wood. Holding this stick and a piece of chasers cement over a flame, heat them both at the same time. As the cement begins to melt, wipe it off on the stick, building up a mound of cement on the end of the stick. Then lay down the cement and pick up the stone with pliers. Hold it and the cement covered lapstick point over the flame and warm them at the same time. As the cement begins to melt and before it quite begins to flow, rub the cement wad against the base of the stone until the base is covered by cement. Then stick the stone onto the stick, and with wet fingers force it into proper position and mold the cement into a symmetrical pyramid about the base of the stone, not allowing it to come quite to the edge. See Fig. 8. The cement and the stone must both be hot. If this job is done carefully, very few stones will come loose from the sticks.

6. *Rough Shaping.*—Put back on the machine the No. 100 carbo wheel and the splash pan. Use the 1500 rpm speed for a

10″ wheel. Holding the stone by its handle, proceed to grind it to its final shape and almost to its final size. This size was

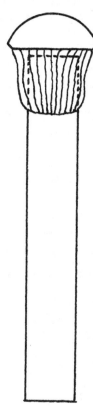

pretty well fixed except as to thickness when the outline was cut. Do all grinding away from the base and toward the top of the crown. One reason is that grinding toward the base might flake the edge of the base. Another reason will be pointed out later.

7. *Smooth Shaping.*—Use No. FF carbo wheel. Speed 800 rpm. A different splash pan and sponge are desirable but not necessary. The surface that was left by the No. 100 wheel is very rough. The wheel cut so fast that there are flat places and ridges on the stone and also scratches and pits. The purpose of this operation is to remove all these irregularities and to give the stone its final shape and size. This is an extremely important operation and should be done carefully. It is the last fast cutting operation, and flaws that may be removed with this wheel in a few seconds will take many minutes of any of the later operations.

Do all grinding here parallel to the base instead of at right angles to the base as was done in the rough shaping. By having the new cuts cross the old ones it is easier to see when the old ones have been entirely ground away. The object of this cut is to entirely cover the face of the stone, not leaving any of the rough ground area with its pits and scratches. The stone must be wiped dry for each inspection. The stone must be kept moving rapidly and pressure must be very light.

Figure 8
LAPSTICK AND STONE ASSEMBLY.
Shows exaggerated working bevel.

8. *Smoothing.*—Put on the same wood wheel that was used for the base and use the same pan of No. FF Carborundum. Speed 400 rpm. It is well to have two or three grooves of varying radii turned in the side of this wheel. Smooth the stone with paste thick and freely applied in the grooves on the side of the wheel. When there are low spots or rough places which do not seem to be disappearing as fast as they should, a few moments on the periphery of the wheel will remove them. Keep the stone moving during this operation but not as fast

as in the former one. Pressure heavy. Job to be continued until there are no rough spots visible under the magnifier.

9. *First Polish.*—This is done with hard felt and pumice or tripoli. Use the same lap and the same reservoir that served for the corresponding operation on the base. Speed 400 rpm. Pressure heavy. Continue until stone seems to have uniform and perfect polish.

10. *Final Polish.*—Do this with tin oxide on hard felt wheel. Same outfit that was used for final polish of base. Same notes apply as applied to final polish on base. Speed 800 rpm. After some use the felt wheel will develop grooves in which the polishing will be done. When these grooves have been formed and polishing can be done in them, considerable pressure may be used as the pressure applied will be distributed over a larger area of contact, but when the lap is new and flat, pressure must be rather light as it is all concentrated on a small arc of contact and will quickly heat the stone at the contact point to where flakes will chip off it and the stone must be recut.

11. *Removing and Cleaning Stone.*—If the gem is of tough material, it can usually be removed from the stick by slipping a knife blade between its base and the wad of cement. But if the structure of the stone, either by nature or through flaws, is weak, such treatment may break the stone. It is safest to always warm the stone and the cement. While they are warming, work the knife blade between cement and the stone, entering it gently and for a short way only, successively on all sides of the stone. When the stone is free from the wad of cement, scrape off the surplus cement with the knife blade and immerse the stone in a bath of alcohol or acetone. The acetone is much faster, softening the cement almost immediately. The alcohol may take 20 minutes, depending much on the kind of cement being used. When the cement is soft, wash the stone well with a cloth wet with alcohol or acetone and wipe with a dry cloth. If the stone has flaws such as in turquoise with matrix, and abrasive has gotten into these flaws, discoloring them, they can be cleaned by washing them with a toothbrush dipped in the alcohol or acetone, striking these places repeatedly with the end of the bristles. Or brief application of the stone to a dry clean wool carpet lap are effective.

General Notes

Size of Batches.—If one were going to produce cabochons commercially, he would have several grinding heads, one for each operation, shielded from each other and driven from a line shaft with pulleys of such size that each head would have its proper speed. For most amateurs this is not practicable or desirable. It calls for too much investment and requires too much space. Most of us get by with a single grinding head and change wheels and speeds as required. In order to lessen as much as possible the labor and time required for such changes, it is well to cut and polish stones in lots instead of individually. Such lots may be of any size at all. It is suggested that the beginner run only two or three at a time and that after he is well under way, this be increased to not less than 10 to 12 stones per batch.

Cementing.—While the technique outlined is intended for use with a single stone, it is applicable to a large number of stones. However, it may prove somewhat easier, when there is a large batch to be cemented, to melt the cement in a seamless vessel over a source of heat such as a cook stove. The stones and sticks may be kept warm in a second pan.

The tip of the stick is dipped in the melted cement, wiped across the base of the stone held with pliers, dipped again, and then the two stuck together and the cement molded to shape with the wet fingers or a wet knife blade. When the lapsticks are once "charged" with cement they may be used over and over with little if any addition of cement. When old sticks are being reused there is no advantage in having the cement melted in a pan, as both stone and cement tipped stick may be so readily warmed over a flame such as an alcohol lamp.

Alcohol Lamp.—An almost indispensable item. Should be used for cementing stones onto sticks and for softening the cement to removes stones from sticks.

Speed Changing.—Should be and can be made easy. If it is not easy, there is too much temptation to use an improper speed to avoid the trouble of changing. Buy three step pulleys for the motor. The grinding head has a shaft projecting from both ends. Use the extension at the left for the driven pulley. Figure out the combination that will give the three speeds required. Have three driven pulleys made of wood at a wood shop or a machine shop, or you can make them yourself. Each of these pulleys is to be just as thick as one of the grooves of the driving pulley. Turn grooves in these wood pulleys for either round or V belt, whichever you propose to use, the latter being the better. Clamp the three wood pulleys together and either bolts or screws may be used for fastening them together into a single three grooved pulley.

Align the driving and the driven pulleys, with motor loose on the work bench. See Fig. 9. Tack or screw a thin strip of wood on each side of the motor base, parallel to the face of

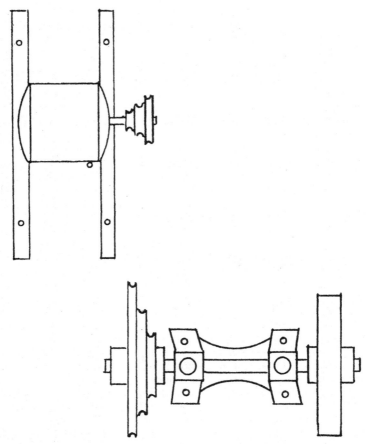

Figure 9.—PLAN. ASSEMBLY OF MOTOR AND GRINDER.
Showing guide strips for motor.

the pulley. This is to act as a guide for the motor when it is moved closer to or further away from the driven pulley. With the belt on a given pair of the pulleys, slide the motor in the groove made by the strips, until the belt is taut. Drill a small hole in the work bench just in front of the motor, and stick a pin such as a large nail in the hole to hold the motor in place. Repeat this procedure for each position the motor will take for the three required speeds.

It will now be the work of only an instant to change speeds

by drawing out a pin, shifting the belt to a new pair of grooves, sliding the motor to its new position and inserting the pin in the new hole.

Location of Grinding Head.—The grinder should be at the front and right of work bench, being sure it is far enough from the edge of the bench to provide good foundation space for the various pans and reservoirs that will be used. The wheel is to revolve downward in front, counterclockwise when facing the grinding head. The work bench should be about 36″ high. A shaded drop light of at least 100 watts should hang where it will shine directly on the work and not in the operator's eyes. It is well to have the drop portable and to provide several positions from which it may hang.

Variety of Lapsticks.—For stones that are not more than twice as long as they are wide, round lapsticks are satisfactory. Round sticks can be bought in a variety of sizes. The cement wad may be built up on opposite sides of the stick to shape of the base of the stone to be cut. But if the stone is very narrow and long it is best to cut a special stick with a tip approximately the shape of the stone. It should be about 1/8″ smaller in all dimensions than the base of the stone. These sticks may be cut with a knife from any wood that is available, old boxes, laths, shingles, etc. The stones that break loose from the sticks are usually the ones that are not supported well at their ends, and it is much easier to support a stone uniformly over all its base on a stick nearly the shape and size of the base than to do the job by building up cement on a stick that is different in shape from the stone.

Holding Stones.—Larger stones, say 3/8″ diameter and up, may be readily held for grinding, by hand. The best technique for holding them will come only with practice. In general such stones are held between the thumbs and forefingers of both hands. In this position it is quite easy to let the nail of the forefinger touch the wheel. When this happens the nail cuts fast and may be seriously cut before the worker is aware of it. Winding a cot of friction tape or ordinary adhesive tape around the tip of the finger affords some protection, but the better scheme is not to depend on this but to be careful and learn to keep the nail away from the wheel. It is difficult to hold stones much smaller than 3/8″ diameter by hand. Such stones should be attached to lapsticks for all cutting both front and rear. For very small stones, say 1/4″ diameter and smaller, wire nails with the heads cut off make excellent lapsticks.

Drying for Inspection.—Almost any ground surface when wet, looks smooth. For this reason it is absolutely necessary that surfaces be wiped dry for inspection.   An easy way to do this is to have a towel, preferably Turkish, hanging from an overhead support, just to one side of the worker's standing position.   The towel should be changed as the work progresses from one step to another to avoid getting coarser abrasives in the finer mixes.   Or the towel, if a large one, may be divided into several "zones," the lower one being used for the coarser grinding and so on to the top, which is used for wiping polished work only.   It is probably better and safer to have separate cloths for each operation.   Ordinary Turkish wash cloths are good for this purpose.

Washing Abrasives from Stones.—The stones and the lapsticks must be washed between operations.   The abrasives hide in irregularities of the cement and the sticks.   An ideal way to wash them is under running water, but if this is not convenient they may be washed in a pail of water using a tooth brush to scrub them.   The same pail of water may be used for all washes if it is not stirred up too much, as the abrasives quickly settle to the bottom.   If this pail of water is kept warm, it will save some breaking loose of stones from the sticks.   The stones will often be dipped in this water during an operation as well as between operations.   The hands should also be washed after the old wheels and pans are taken away and before the new ones are put in place.

Cements.—Ordinary sealing wax may be used as cement if the base of the stone is first coated with melted shellac.   The shellac may be applied either from a stick of shellac wiped, while partially melted, across the base of the warm stone, or, when the stone is warm, the liquid shellac may be applied with a brush. It dries almost instantly on a warm stone.   Some lapidaries use a cement made of equal parts of sealing wax and marine glue. Others use a cement made by mixing sealing wax and shellac in equal parts.   Others mix powdered pumice with chasers cement. But for ordinary cabochon work the ordinary chasers cement will usually be found satisfactory.

Water Feed for Grinding.—If one is rigging up a permanent grinder in a fixed location it doubtless pays to use a gravity feed for the water supply.   This is done by installing at an elevated location, a reservoir, which may be an ordinary sheet metal bucket, with a drip valve and a tube, either metal or rubber or both, from the reservoir to a point beneath the shield where the drip will fall on the face of the wheel.

When all operations are to be done on one head, this scheme may or may not pay, and the determination of it must be left to the individual.

Dressing of Wheels.—Carborundum wheels will wear out of true. Sometimes this happens with annoying frequency, sometimes they will run true for a long time. When they become too eccentric, they not only do not cut fast enough but they may pound the stone that is being ground until it comes loose from the stick. Before they reach this extreme condition they should be trued with a wheel dresser. A diamond embedded in the end of a steel rod is available for truing, but it costs more than most amateurs care to spend for such a device and the ordinary "emery wheel dresser," consisting of a series of steel discs free turning in a convenient holder, costs little and is entirely satisfactory. The dresser must be held firmly on the tool rest. The wheel should be run at its highest safe speed as given by the manufacturer. Much faster cutting will result if the tool is held slightly sidewise so that its discs are not quite parallel to the wheel.

Flatting of Wheels.—The tendency to develop flats is much less if the wheel is operated at the highest safe speed. Flat places are often caused by heavy pressure of sharp edges or points of a stone against the wheel. If only a few extra grains of carborundum are torn loose from the wheel at one particular point, the slight depression may start the stone to bumping at this point and rapidly dig a deep hole in the wheel.

It should be kept in mind that it is not necessary nor desirable to true the wheel immediately on its beginning to bump. Sometimes, though not often, the bumping will disappear or at least will fail to become more violent, and the user should at least wait and give the wheel a chance to correct itself.

Carborundum Wheels—Hardness of.—These instructions all refer to the No. 100 wheel as being of "J" hardness. Lapidaries, both amateur and professionals, have their own ideas as to what hardness is best, and all grades from and including "J" through "K" and "L" to and including "M" are used. The "J" wheel is the hardest of this series and the "M" wheel is the softest. In selecting the desired hardness of wheel keep in mind that the softer wheels cut the gem faster and wear themselves away faster than the harder wheels. If a Carborundum wheel did not wear away, it would quickly become glazed and refuse to cut. It is through the pulling away of worn grains and the constant exposing of new sharp grains that it is enabled to cut at a fairly constant speed. The faster it wears away the old dull grains, the faster it exposes new sharp grains and the faster it cuts the gem. If one were producing gems commercially, his time would have a definite value and it would doubtless pay to use the softer, faster cutting wheel, but if one is pursuing gem cutting only

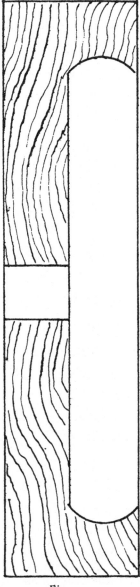

Figure 10
INTERNAL GRINDER—
SECTION.
Should be about 8" dia.,
1 3/4" thick.

as a hobby and places no particular value on his time, the harder wheel is the more economical. Also it should be considered that the softer wheels are more subject to flatting.

Control of Splash.—The degree to which this is necessary or desirable depends on a good many things but especially on the location of the outfit. Perfect control is almost impossible. If the outfit is located in a basement or an outhouse, it may be preferable not to bother too much about splashing. If the machine is located where the water will injure surrounding objects, it is of course necessary to do what can be done to keep the splash confined. Under such circumstances it is well to place a large pan under the splash pan assembly and to hang cloth aprons from the metal shield of the splash pan. These can hang down in front of the shield to where they touch the wheel, and on the sides of the wheel they may hang down into the reservoir. Some experimenting will enable the user to make these quite effective. So place them that they cannot get tangled with the revolving wheel or spindle.

Internal Grinder.—This has been widely used for the wood and carbo operation which is Step 8 in the routine given in this chapter. This device is as pictured in Fig. 10. The principle is right. The carbo mix is held in place by centrifugal force and works much faster than if applied to the side or the periphery of a wheel. But for some reasons these grinders get "bumpy" very quickly, and when they do so it is necessary to chuck them in a lathe to re-true them. For this reason there is some doubt of its value and it may be best to use the slower but cheaper and less troublesome plain wood wheel with grooves on its side.

Alternate to Cast Iron Lap.—If one wishes to avoid buying a cast iron lap, and expects to do no flatting except the small bases of cabochon cut stones, he can make a very satisfactory substitute with a piece of sheet tin or zinc and a wood wheel. Put the plain flat wood wheel on the arbor, slip a tin or zinc disc against it and tighten the arbor nut to hold the metal disc in place. It is not necessary to fasten the metal to the wood. In fact it is best not to so fasten it. It is often desired to take a stone away from this lap with a sliding motion out to and over the edge. If the metal is fastened to the wood, the screw or nail projecting through prevents the use of this useful movement. This scheme is not nearly so good as a cast iron lap but is usable.

Soap for Mixing Pastes.—In all pastes made of abrasives and water the abrasives tend to settle quickly to the bottom of the mix. Also the paste after being applied to the lap, having nothing but water to hold it, tends to fly off the lap. These conditions can be considerably improved by the addition of soap to the mix. Any readily soluble soap is satisfactory. Chip soap is more easily used than soap cakes. "Gardinol W. A. Powder" is especially recommended. It is a synthetic soap powder made by the National Analine and Chemical Co.

Messrs. Kress and Woolworth.—The amateur gem cutter can hardly go into a "Ten Cent Store" without finding something he needs. Among the items he can buy here and often at a considerable saving over buying them elsewhere are: small tools, oil cloth, sponges, paint brushes, tooth brushes, metal pans and pails, towels, wash cloths and so forth.

Cheaper Felt Wheels.—This is mentioned as an alternate not to be adopted if there is any way out of it, but only to be tried if the buying of the correct wheels is utterly impossible. Felt wheels 1" x 6" are quite expensive. An ideal equipment would embrace 4 of them, one for pumice on flat bases, one for tin oxide on flat bases, one (with grooves worn in the periphery) for pumice on curved surfaces, and one with grooves for tin oxide. Most of us do not feel able or justified in making such an investment. The 1" x 6" wheel is practically a necessity for the pumice polishes. However, a satisfactory substitute for use with the tin oxide for final polishes is a felt wheel 1/4" thick x 6" diameter installed against the side of a flat wood wheel. The polishing will then be done on the flat side of the felt instead of on its periphery.

Linotile Laps.—Linotile is a hard linoleum used by some

amateurs for polishing large flats. It will stand heavy pressure and is also good for small flats. It is an interesting material and worth experimenting with.

Battleship Linoleum.—Used by some amateurs instead of wood for smoothing cabochons. Used with FF powder. Is low priced and a number of discs may be kept with various shapes ánd sizes of grooves. Use against the side of a wood wheel.

Wool Carpet.—Sometimes used in place of felt for both the pumice and tin oxide polishes. Use against the side of a wood wheel.

Leather Laps.—Useful for polishing soft cabochons or for material with soft matrix. When the matrix tends to be dragged out by a felt wheel, the leather, preferably buckskin or sheepskin, will usually be more satisfactory for a final polish. Use on the side of a wood wheel. If it is to be used for flats, install it directly against the side of the flat wood wheel. If it is to be used for curved surfaces, turn some shallow grooves in the side of the wood wheel, then tack the leather tight on the wheel and do the polishing directly over the grooves. Or, put back of the leather, a pad of felt or sponge rubber or several thicknesses of cloth. In either case tack the leather to the wheel. For polishing flats with leather, a wood wheel about 2″ thick with the leather cemented to its periphery is convenient, it then being called a "drum polisher." It is especially suitable for large flats. Either tin oxide or powdered rouge may be used with the leather polishers.

Shapes of Cabochons.—Generally, cabochon shaped stones are cut with a curved front and a flat base. If the material is strictly opaque, here is no need for any departure from this rule. If the material is transparent, it is usually best to cut it "double cabochon," with curved front and back so as to get a better return of light. If the material is translucent and pleasing in color but very dark in color, good results may often be gotten by hollowing out the base, making the stone virtually a shell of whatever thickness gives the best color. This hollowing of the back may best be done with a diamond drill. Cement the stone to a wood block of size convenient to handle. Hold it loosely in the hands, feeding it "freehand" to the drill revolving in the drill press. By careful manipulation a symmetrical hollow can be formed. It can be sufficiently polished with wood pins with rounded ends, chucked in the drill press, using Carborundum paste as the abrasive. Be careful not to overheat the stone.

Permissible shapes for cabochon gems are unlimited. A few are given in Fig. 11. A collection of gems, all other factors being identical, is much improved in appearance if it is made up of a wide variety of shapes and sizes. Window shopping at jewelry stores and close observation of shapes seen there is helpful.

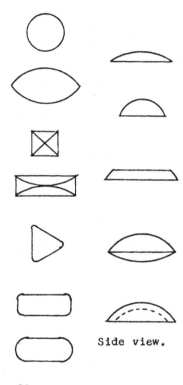

Side view.

Plan.

Figure 11.—Cabochon Shapes. Hundreds of variations and combinations can be worked out from these basic shapes.

Curved versus Flat Surfaces. —Curved surfaces are much easier to cut and polish than are flat ones. On the curved surface of a gem stone no exact fixed shape is to be attained, and so the taking out of a fault by additional grinding is entirely permissible and, if the fault is of reasonable depth only, will not change the shape of the stone far enough from the ideal to be noticeable. This is not true of a flat surface. If a fault shows up on a flat surface, the entire surface must be lowered uniformly to the depth of the fault.

Speeding the Pumice Polish. —Step 9 in the routine may be considerably speeded up by the addition of about 10 percent of No. 600 Carborundum powder. Note that this is not recommended for soft stones, because while it will speed this operation it will leave scratches that will take an undue time to remove with the tin oxide in the following final polish.

Pumice v e r s u s Tripoli.— These have been referred to as being interchangeable. That is the case. Some users prefer one, some prefer the other.

Grade of Pumice.—There seems to be no fixed standard of grading or designation. Pumice that is sold in drug stores for household cleaning is too fine for general use. It works too slowly though giving excellent results on very soft stones. The correct material for stones such as agate and jasper has the feel of very fine sand.

Sanding—An Alternate to Wood Wheel Smoothing.—Many users prefer a "sanding" device to the wood wheel for Routine Step 8. There are several, or rather many, ways in which this can be made. One of these ways is what has been written up as a "Sunflower Lap," so called from the appearance of the backing of the sanding disc. See Fig. 12. This is made as

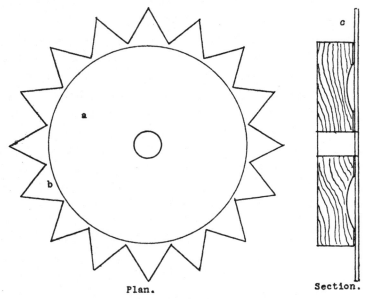

Plan.   Section.

Figure 12.—SUNFLOWER SANDING LAP.

Emery cloth (a) glued to rubber disc (b). Tips (c) to be folded back on edge of wheel and held in place with rubber band.

---

follows: Buy discs of No. 180 or No. 220 Carborundum cloth about 6″ dia. or buy sheets of this cloth and cut out such discs. Cut a large sheet of soft rubber from the inner tire of an automobile. This should be about 9″ dia. Serrate the edges as shown in the sketch. The diameter of the rubber disc at the bottom of the serrations should be equal to or a little greater than the diameter of the sanding disc. Install this assembly on the side of a wood wheel about 1 1/2″ thick and with a diameter about equal to the diameter of the rubber disc at the bottom of its serrations. Provide a rubber band about 1″ wide by cutting off a section of the inner tube. Cut holes for the arbor in the center of the rubber disc and in the center of the cloth disc. The cloth disc is attached to the rubber disc by wetting it thoroughly and placing it against the rubber disc and putting under pressure overnight. There is glue enough in the cloth to cause it to adhere to the rubber. Or it may be glued to the rubber disc with ordinary Carborundum glue and left under pressure over night. Turn a groove in the side of the wood wheel as shown in the sketch. After the cloth has hardened in place on the rubber disc, place the wood wheel and the rubber disc together on the arbor of the grinder and tighten the arbor nut. Fold the "ears" of the rubber disc back on the periphery of the wood wheel, using the rubber band to hold them in place and leave the rubber band on them. If the band going once around the wheel is not tight enough, it must be stretched and given a half twist and put twice around the wheel.

Or the rubber band may be omitted and a metal band used instead. If this is done, taper the edge of the wood wheel so that the band will draw tight.

Or the rubber band and the "ears" on the rubber disc may be omitted and the rubber disc fastened to the wood wheel with tacks which are easily drawn when discs are worn and are to be changed. It is best to make several discs at a time.

Another way to make the sander is to cement the cushion (rubber, soft felt, cloth or leather) to the wood wheel and install the cloth loose on this, the cloth being held in place by tacks or by having its edge folded back over the rim of the wheel and held by a metal band. There does not seem to be any overwhelming merit in either scheme over the other.

This sanding operation works perfectly when the cloth is in perfect condition. The cloth when first put in service is likely to be too coarse and must be broken in by holding against it a piece of stone while it revolves at normal speed. It then, during its life, passes through a stage when it is perfect. Then it begins to be too dull and slow and finally is discarded. One objection to the sander is that its period of perfect condition is of too short duration. This objection is largely answered by the use of loose sheets on a cushioned back cemented to the wood, thereby making negligible the work of changing discs. Another objection is that if the cement with which the stone is held to the stick, gets on the carbo cloth, it forms a glaze that stops cutting. It is often impossible to so carefully form the cement around the base of the stone that it will not be cut by this sander when work is being done close to the base of the stone. This objection comes in the class with the last one mentioned; it is not serious if it is easy to change to a new cloth when an old one is spoiled.

Another objection mentioned, the shortness of life of the "perfect condition," is somewhat met by some shops by having two of these sanders, one more worn than the other. The stones are treated first with the less worn sander and finished on the one with the greater amount of wear. When it is too smooth for further use, it is discarded, the less worn one takes its place, and a new one is broken in for the first operation.

The speed of the sander is about 1500 rpm and the pressure very light. Heating will result if much pressure is used. The stone must be kept moving with a twisting motion to prevent grinding of flat places as well as to prevent excessive heating in one spot.

The Carborundum surface on a worn cloth can be renewed by coating the surface with a thin layer of silicate of soda and dusting on it the proper carbo powder. Use a sieve for this. Shake off the excess, let stand over night, and the disc is again ready for use after the "breaking in" already mentioned.

The relative merits of the sanding operation and the same work done with a wood wheel as outlined in Routine Step 8 are debatable. Either is satisfactory. Often a combination of the two is worth while, using the sander first to smooth out irregularities in the stone, then the wood wheel to give a finer finish.

Hardness of Lap—Effect of.—The beginner will find some mystifying results as he experiments with laps and abrasives of varying hardness. The speed of polishing and the degree of polish attained in a given operation depend on: the hardness of the stone, the hardness of the lap, and the hardness of the abrasive. None of these can be changed without changing the result of the operation. In dealing with a given stone we cannot change its hardness nor nature, but we can use an unlimited number of combinations of laps and abrasives. A notable example of behavior that will appear peculiar to the beginner is shown in the Routine outlined in this chapter where the base of a stone is flatted with No. 600 carbo on an iron lap and no hint of a polish appears, but when this is followed with the much coarser No. FF carbo on a wood lap, a considerable degree of polish results. The treatment outlined in the Routine is designed for stones of the hardness of agate but is also suitable for stones as soft as Malachite, except that the final polish on the softer stones is best done with a soft felt lap or a sheepskin lap. Each worker must find by experience what combinations give him the best results.

Special Treatments—Opal.—Certain opals, especially some of those from the Western United States of America, tend to crack when being cut and polished. Changes in temperature and physical shock are probably the factors responsible for this. Precautions that will help to overcome this trouble are:

1. Saw only with a diamond saw, run it at rather low speed, and feed slowly to avoid heating.

2. In heating the stone to attach it to the lapstick put it in lukewarm water over a fire and bring the water to the temperature desired.

3. Use warm water in the reservoir when cutting and for mixing all pastes.

4. Do all work slowly to avoid heating.

5. After polishing, keep all such especially fragile stones coated with or immersed in glycerine to keep them from drying out and cracking.

Special Treatment—Turquoise in Matrix.—This same treatment is applicable to all soft stones in matrix when the matrix consists of loosely cemented grains of hard material that tend to come loose and scratch the gem material during polishing. Of such stones, turquoise, variscite and amatrice are notable. Handle them in the standard way up to the final polishing operation, then instead of polishing with tin oxide on a felt lap, use either tin oxide or rouge on a leather lap. Use the smooth side of a leather such as sheepskin or buckskin. The felt, being rough, digs down into the matrix and loosens grains of it which either roll across or are dragged across the gem surfaces. The final pumice treatment does this, leaving the matrix slightly undercut. The leather, being smooth, polishes the high spots of gem material without disturbing the matrix. The abrasive in this operation sticks in irregularities of the matrix and must be washed out with a stiff brush and alcohol or acetone.

Special Treatment—Very Soft Stones.—Many very soft stones will not show a good polish when finished with either the tin oxide and felt lap scheme or the leather and tin oxide process. There are several schemes that may be tried on such stones and usually one or another of them will give good results.

Some of them will yield to pumice or tripoli if used on a dry felt lap followed by tin oxide on a dry felt lap.

There are two kinds of muslin wheels, one is sewed and the other unsewed. The unsewed wheel will not permit much pressure, as the sheets of cloth separate when any appreciable pressure is applied to its periphery. The sewed lap permits the use of considerably more pressure before it begins to buckle and turn to one side.

There are several soft abrasives available for use on these laps. Among them are:

Tin Oxide
Red Rouge in powder form
Red Rouge in stick form
Green Rouge
Whiting
Prepared Chalk

Some one of these agents on one or the other of the cloth laps, used either wet or dry, will solve most polishing problems on very soft stones.

There are stones both hard and soft that will not take polish or will take only a very imperfect one. Be sure the stone is not one of this kind before using too much effort on it.

Special Treatment—Corundum Cabochons.—Star sapphires are the principal stones using this treatment. There are also the star rubies, of which amateurs get very few, and there are some opaque blue and pink corundums as well as other colors that should be treated in this way.

1. *Roughing Out.*—This may be done on a 100 J carbo wheel at 1500 rpm. This wears a Corborundum wheel at a terrific rate though it is the fastest cutting scheme of the two that will be outlined. An alternate slower but much cheaper way is to grind them on the side of a cast iron wheel, using a paste of water and No. 100 carbo grains. The speed should be from 200 to 400 rpm, slow enough to prevent the excessive throwing of the paste. Pressure should be very heavy.

2. *Second Cut.*—May be done with an FF carbo wheel or with FF paste on the side of a cast iron wheel. The same notes apply as to the previous paragraph, the carbo wheel is faster, the iron wheel is cheaper. The same cast iron wheel may be used for the two operations by washing it after using with the No. 100 paste.

3. *First Smoothing.*—Use FF carbo paste on the side of a lead lap with speed of 800 rpm and heavy pressure. This will result in some heating and therefore must be watched for this. This is not a fast cutting operation, but is important and should be continued until it is sure no further improvement in surface condition can be noted.

4. *Second Smoothing.*—This step can be and often is omitted. Some users insist it is well worth while. It consists of a duplication of step 3 except using No. 600 carbo paste instead of No. FF. Little change in appearance of the surface

will be visible; so the step must be blindly continued for a reasonable time, and care must be taken that all parts of the stone are covered by this grind.

5. *Polishing.*—This is done on a copper lap. Cold rolled rectangular bars are suitable for the making of this lap. It may be 1/4″ x 5″. The lap must be initially well scored and must be kept in this condition. See Fig. 13. The deep scratches on the lap can be made with a heavy knife or with the corner or point of a file or with a sharp corner of a broken hacksaw blade. They should be about 1/4″ apart at the periphery. Run this lap at 800 rpm. Keep the surface well daubed with a heavy paste of either tripoli or rottenstone. (I have not found any appreciable difference in the behavior of the two abrasives for this purpose). Do not let the lap run dry. Use moderate pressure.

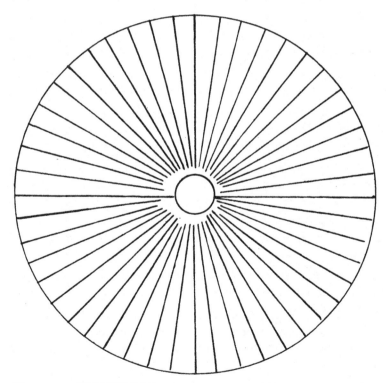

Figure 13.—COPPER LAP.
Scored for polishing Corundum.

6. *General Discussion.*—Star sapphires need not have their backs polished. The backs should be ground only to a fair symmetry. As much material as possible should be left in the backs, as this strengthen the star.

In cutting star sapphires there may be some trouble in properly orienting the finished cut so that the star is in its center. This may be done by "cut and try" rule. Cement the stone on the lap stick in what appears to be about the correct position, assuming that the girdle will be at right angles to the stick. Grind a small curved area at what will be the peak of the crown. Dry the stone and dip in cedar oil or cinnamon oil and inspect under a concentrated light. Have the light directly over the observer's head, hold the stone directly in front with the lapstick vertical and the stone pointed directly toward the light. The star will now be visible, and by moving the lapstick and watching the moving of the star it is possible to see about how much the stone should be shifted in the cement to bring the star to the center of the stone. Now turn the stick 90 degrees in the fingers and make the same tests and observations. Soften the cement with heat, shift the stone the amount and direction you think will make it right, dip in the oil and test again. Several adjustments may be necessary to locate the star positively in the center of the stone, but after this has been done, the only care to be taken is to cut the stone symmetrical to the lapstick. Stars are either not visible or are very faint in greatly diffused light. It is therefore impossible to inspect them in daylight in an open space. They are best seen at night under a single strong light. When they must be inspected in the daytime, they should be placed in the bottom of a deep inclosure such as a cylinder of heavy paper, preferably black, just large enough to enable a strong light to be directed on them and at the same time to permit observation.

The beginner should not use a good stone for his first effort. Good rough star sapphires are hard to find, and practice should be done on an inferior stone. This job is slow in all its stages, especially the polishing. The polishing operation must be carefully guarded against admission of coarse abrasives such as Carborundum.

When these stones are produced commercially, they are cut with a diamond charged lap. As few amateurs have such laps, or can justify their purchase for their limited needs, no discussion of them will be given. Norbide is very effective in cutting corundum.

Special Treatment—Jade.—A typical piece of jade is not of uniform hardness throughout. It is nearly enough uniform that all parts of it will take a polish, but the soft sections will be undercut, giving the surface a "lumpy" appearance. It is generally left this way, which is entirely satisfactory for a large carving. But if a fine piece of this material is to be made into a set for a ring, for example, it deserves a finer finish than can be gotten with the regular routine laid down for cabochons.

This finer and flatter finish may be given it at the cost of some extra time. Put the stone through all the steps of the regular routine up to and including the polish. Follow the regular tin oxide and felt wheel polish with a polish with tin oxide on a leather lap such as was described for use on turquoise in matrix. This, as remarked, will give all areas a perfect polish but will leave the stone "bumpy." These bumps are now taken off down to the level of the lowest places by polishing with a thick paste of tin oxide on the side of a tin lap, using a speed of 800 rpm with moderate pressure. This is a slow job but well repays the effort put in it if the stone is worthy of cutting in this form and of being put to this purpose.

*Special Treatment—Grossularite.—*There is a beautiful form of this material, known as "South African Jade," that behaves just as was noted of jade in the former paragraph and yields to the same treatment.

*Time Requirements.—*The time required to cut and polish a a cabochon cut stone varies with many factors, such as hardness of stone, size of stone, adequacy of equipment, skill of cutter, degree of perfection of finish and form demanded, etc. Stones of ordinary size and ordinary hardness should require an average time of 30 to 40 minutes after the cutter has had some experience. It is worth reiterating here that each step in the routine should be carried to its limit without skimping. Each step is designed to accomplish just one thing, to bring the stone more nearly to its final shape and finish. Each step is a slower cutting step than the one that preceded it. Any work that should be done by a given operation is done with a minimum of effort by that operation. If the work is skimped in any given step it will require several times as long to do it in a later step.

CHAPTER III

LARGE FLATS

We are not concerned with very large flats such as slabs of building marbles and slates, etc. The cutting of these is necessarily a commercial enterprise and the technique may be observed and learned at any marble yard.

Often it is desired to polish large surfaces such as one foot square and larger on mineral specimens for museums and for private collections. When this is to be done, it should be turned over to some specialist who is equipped to do it economically, as the amateur will usually not have enough such work to justify the necessary expenditure for equipment.

The work that the amateur is concerned with is the polishing of medium sized slabs of sizes from 2″ up to say 6″ or 8″, such as are required to properly display sections through small agate nodules and miscellaneous slabs for the ordinary private collection and for the making of ornamental objects such as book ends, ashtrays, paper weights, etc.

The smaller of such objects up to several inches in diameter may be worked on the ordinary amateur's standard equipment, such as he uses for the flat backs of cabochons. He should by all means have a cast iron lap about 8″ to 10″ in diameter, but lacking this he can use a sheet tin or zinc or iron disc against the side of a wood wheel.

Routine No. I.—Saw slab to required thickness with a mud saw or a diamond saw. The diamond saw gives a much cleaner and flatter cut than the mud saw, leaving much less work to be done by grinding.

Grind flat with No. 150 carbo made into a paste with water, on the side of a 10″ cast iron lap. Speed about 800 rpm.

Repeat this grind with same speed and same lap, using No. FF carbo. Wash all the No. 150 carbo off the lap and off the material before applying the No. FF paste. If the surface is fairly smooth from the sawing, the No. 150 operation may be omitted.

Grind further with paste of No. 600 carbo, using a different lap or the reverse side of the lap used for the coarser work. It is permissible, but not advisable, to use the same lap as was used for the coarser jobs, but if this is done, extreme care must be exercised that all the coarse grains of carbo are washed off before this operation begins. Continue this grind until the whole surface when dry presents a uniform appearance. Give especial attention to the edges, which tend to be rounded slightly.

The smoothing is done on the periphery of a maple wheel, 2″ thick x 10″ dia. with a paste of No. FF carbo with water. Use speed of about 400 rpm and heavy pressure. The stone must be kept moving during this job, in a direction parallel to the rotation of the wheel. If the stone is held still, the relatively fast cutting wood lap will grind a hollow in the flat surface, and this will show at least in distorted reflections when the stone is polished. It is well to work out a definite pattern of movement for this operation and all the following ones, and to adhere strictly to this pattern until the use of it becomes a habit. With the wheel daubed with paste and turning downward on the edge next to the worker, the flat is to be placed against the periphery of the wheel. See Fig. 14. But the top edge of the flat must not be placed against the wheel, as it would scrape the abrasive off the wheel. Apply to the wheel a spot on the stone a little below the top edge. Then at a slow but uniform speed, move the stone upward until the arc of contact has traveled to the lower edge and off the stone, with a little extra stress on the lower

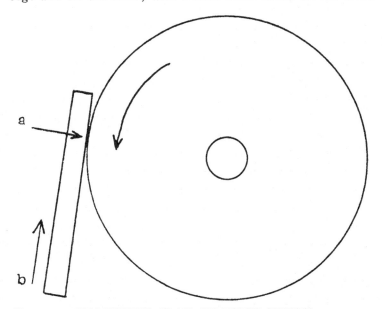

Figure 14.—SMOOTHING FLAT ON WOOD WHEEL.
a. Establish contact at this point.
b. Move work in this direction.

edge of the stone. If the stone is wider than the face of the wheel, move it over and repeat this travel until all parts of the face have been covered except the narrow strip at the top edge. Now turn the stone 90° and repeat the operation. Then two more moves of 90° each, when the whole surface will have been covered. Wipe the surface dry and examine it. Where imperfect smoothing is found, apply again to the wheel and smooth such spots, remembering to keep the stone moving.

The first polish is done on the periphery of a hard felt wheel. Such wheels as owned by most amateurs are 1″ x 6″ and these are entirely satisfactory, though necessarily slower cutting than a larger thicker wheel. Use a paste of either tripoli or pumice with water. Speed 400 rpm. Pressure heavy. If the stone is a very hard one such as agate or jasper, the polishing may be speeded up by the addition of about 10 percent of No. 600 carbo powder to the tripoli or pumice. It does not pay to use this mixture on the softer stones, as it will leave on them scratches that are hard to remove in the final polishing. This operation is to be continued until a uniformly smooth, fairly well polished surface is apparent. Use the same pattern of travel as was used for the wood wheel.

The real and final polish is given on a similar wheel using paste of tin oxide. Speed 800 rpm. Pressure medium. Keep stone moving as in previous operations.

Routine No. II.—This is for larger stones such as would require unduly large laps if treated as in Routine No. I.

A grinder such as is used by opticians for grinding lenses is most convenient for this work. This has a vertical spindle, and the laps, which may be bought from the makers of the machines, fit on the tapered top end of the spindle and have no arbor projecting through their face. But such outfits cost more than most amateurs care to spend for equipment that would be used only occasionally. Those who do invest in such machines can readily adapt the routine given herein to their machines, but feeling that most amateurs will have only grinders with horizontal spindles, the routine given will be based on the use of such machines.

The prime requisite in this scheme is to have a lap, the whole surface of which is available for work and that does not have an arbor and nut projecting through its face to render all its central part unusable. Such a lap is shown in Fig. 15 and is actually an ordinary face plate made to fit the arbor of the particular machine on which it is to be used. It should be about 10″ dia. It must have bearing enough on the spindle to make it run at least fairly true. It should be made and machined in

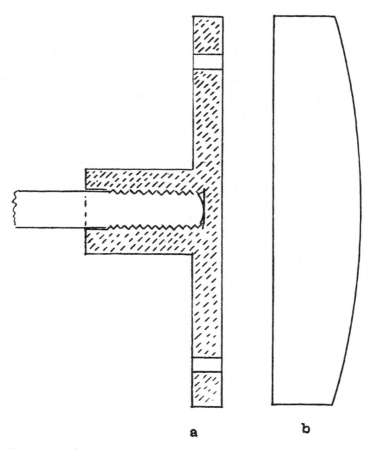

a   b

Figure 15.—FACE PLATE FOR LARGE FLATS.
    a. Section through cast iron face plate.
    b. Wood lap—crown exaggerated—to be attached to cast
        iron plate.

local foundry and shop. It is well to have several of these made, the exact number to be determined after a reading of the rest of this chapter.

The slab is first sawed with diamond or mud saw.

One of the cast iron special laps or "face plates" is then used to grind the slab flat with No. 150 carbo paste. Speed 800 rpm. Or 400 rpm may be better if the slab is large.

Repeat with No. FF carbo paste on the same lap, being sure that all the coarser carbo has been washed off the lap and the stone.

Repeat again with No. 600 carbo paste. A separate lap is better but is not essential if the present one is washed carefully.

The smoothing can be done on such a maple lap as was used in Routine No. I and many users prefer to use such a lap. However, others prefer to take one of the face plates that has holes in it and attach to its face a lap of maple wood and do the smoothing on this plate in the same position as was used for the grinding. The wood lap should be turned with a little crown to it and be anchored to the face plate with wood screws. For the smoothing use a paste of water and No. FF carbo. Speed 400 rpm. Pressure heavy.

The polishing lap is made exactly as was the wood smoothing lap with the addition of a felt pad glued to the face of the wood disc. This felt should be hard and at least 1/8" thick and is applied with ordinary Carborundum glue applied hot and allowed to set over night with the felt held to the wood disc by pressure. The abrasive is a paste of water and either tripoli or pumice. As noted in Routine No. I, if the material is very hard, the polishing may be speeded up by adding 10 percent of No. 600 carbo to the mix, but this should not be done on stones softer than agate. Speed 400 rpm. Pressure heavy.

The final polish as was suggested for the first polish can be done either on such a felt wheel as was used for the same operation in Routine No. I, or on a felt lap which is an exact duplicate of the one used for the first polish in this Routine No. II. Tin oxide and water paste is the polishing medium, and the speed can be raised to 800 rpm. Pressure medium.

Notes—In Routine No. II it is suggested that to avoid having so many of the cast iron face plates, one plate be used for all grinding and another plate with holes in it be used for all other operations. Using this scheme involves changing wood discs on the face plate for each change of operations, instead of changing face plates each time. This is not vastly more trouble and appreciably lowers the necessary investment.

Many combinations and variations of the above outlines are possible and are used. Often the exact procedure is determined by the equipment available. And often routines so determined are equally effective. For example, some cutters do not use the wood wheel for smoothing but use instead a hard felt wheel with No. FF carbo paste. Others omit this step entirely, going directly from carbo on iron lap to pumice or tripoli on felt.

Canvas is sometimes used as a vehicle for the pumice or tripoli instead of felt.

Discarded Sampson Cloth from billiard tables is sometimes used instead of felt. It is glued to the wood just as was done with the felt.

Some users have the face plate for polishing machined with a slight crown and glue the felt directly on it. This is wholly effective but prevents using a single face plate for several operations.

On stone as hard as agate or jasper, the polish that is given by the pumice or tripoli is often satisfactory. But invariably it can be much heightened by the use of the final polish with tin oxide.

Soft stones such as malachite show better polish if treated finally with soft felt instead of the hard felt specified for general use with the final polish. These soft stones are often further improved if given a final polish on the periphery of a cloth buffing wheel with paste of tin oxide. Some are further improved if the cloth buffing wheel polish is concluded with the cloth dry.

CHAPTER IV

GEM DRILLING
General Discussion

The amateur often wants to drill beads and pendants. If the material of which such objects are made is of the softer minerals, they may be drilled with steel drills. This applies to malachite, turquoise, etc., and even obsidian may be drilled with a steel drill if the work is submerged in turpentine. The drill best suited for this work is shown in Fig. 16. It is made by flatting, at its end, a piece of steel rod, grinding it to shape and giving the point a glass hard temper. This drill is not suitable for very small holes, as its use requires considerable pressure, and if made too small, its shank will buckle under this pressure. Ordinary twist drills are also suitable for the very soft minerals.

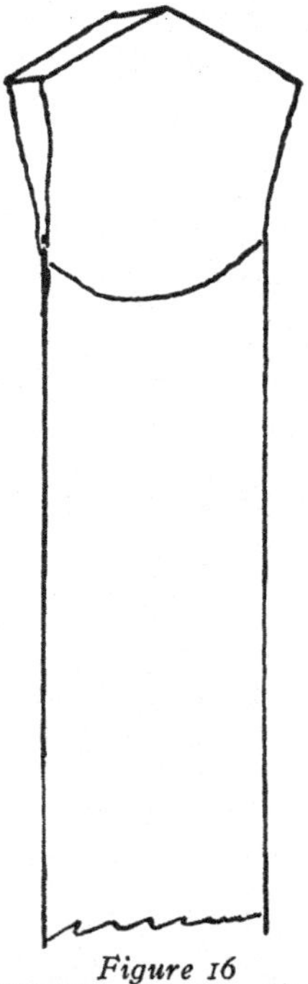

Figure 16
STEEL DRILL FOR SOFT STONES.

For the harder stones some other medium than steel must be used. If the hole is quite large, say 1/8" or larger, Carborundum powder may be used with a tube drill such as described later for use with diamond dust. When this is done the Carborundum is fed continually to the point of the tube in the form of a paste made with water. But this procedure is very slow and cuts a very coarse hole and is to be used only as a last resort.

The only satisfactory way to drill such holes as the gem cutter usually wants is with diamond as the cutting medium. For the sake of clarifying instrucctions there will be described the several distinct methods of directing the diamond to its work. The range of size of hole to which each type of drill is especially applicable is wholly arbitrary.

Large Tube Drills.—This type of drill should be used for holes from 3/16" up. It differs from the later described "small tube drill" in that the end of it is nicked and the large grains of diamond are driven forcibly into its point instead of using small grains embedded by pressure only. The tool consists of a tube attached to a shank suitable for chucking in a drill press. See Fig. 17. The end of the tube is nicked with a knife, the knife blade being driven into the metal with light taps of a hammer. Fairly coarse diamond dust is mixed with olive oil or castor oil and smeared over the end of the tube and driven into the nicks with light hammer blows. The material may be copper, brass or steel. The drill must be true, and for that reason it pays to make it all in one piece on a lathe. The speed of the drill press may vary from 400 rpm to 1000 rpm. The pressure should be rather light. Cutting should be lubricated with plenty of kerosene, but it is not necessary to submerge the work in kerosene.

Small Tube Drills.—This scheme is indicated on holes from the smallest the amateur will drill, probably about the size of an ordinary pin, up to 3/16″. The drill differs from the "large tube drill" already described in that it uses small grains of dia-

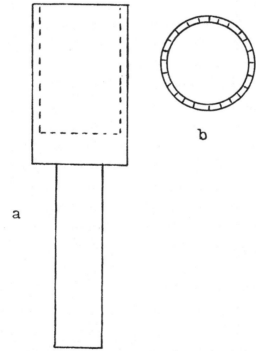

Figure 17.—LARGE TUBE DRILL.
a. Side view.
b. End view showing nicks.

mond and these are forced into the material of the drill by pressure only. It is essentially the same in operation as the large tube drill. Manufacturers of jewelers findings can supply these small drawn tubes and they may be bought through local jewelers. Sterling silver is a suitable material of which to have them made. In use they differ from the large tube drill in the method of application of the diamond. The smaller tubes are too frail to stand any hammering. They also require a finer grade of dust than was used for the large drill, because the walls of the tube are quite thin. In buying dust indicate what size drill it is to be used with and the manufacturer can furnish the correct size of dust.

Mix the dust to a paste with olive oil or castor oil. Anchor the work in position on the bed plate of the drill press. It is well to cement it to a block and fasten the block to the bed plate. Chuck the small tube, letting it extend from the chuck only slightly more than the depth of hole to be drilled. With a small wood point such as a tooth pick, daub a small amount of paste on the work at the point where the drill will enter the work. Bring the drill down forcibly against this daub of paste several times, turning the drill between its touches to the work. The purpose of this is to drive the grains of diamond into the end of the tube. The frailty of the tube must be kept in mind, and the striking of the point against the work must not be heavy enough to bend the tube. Then start up the drill press and keep the cutting lubricated with kerosene. The pressure must be very light, especially on the smaller sizes. When the charge is lost, the drill is lifted out of the hole, a small amount of the paste is inserted in the hole, or daubed on the end of the tube, and the drill (not revolving) is brought down against the work several times as was done for the initial charge. The speed may be anything at all within reason so long as the work is not allowed to get too hot. From 500 to 2000 rpm is suitable.

The Diamond Drill.—This drill is made by embedding either one or two pieces of carbon (black diamond) in the end of a steel rod in such a way that it, or they, project just past the end and the sides of the rod. See Fig. 18. This type of drill is especially suitable for holes from 3/32″ to 3/16″ in size. On such sizes of holes it is much faster than the tube drills and if handled carefully has unlimited life. When made in smaller sizes it is too frail for general use. Holes larger than 3/16″ are quite readily drilled with the large tube drill.

Neither the drill with the one diamond nor that with two diamonds is in all respects superior to the other. Each has its advantages and its disadvantages. The drill with the single

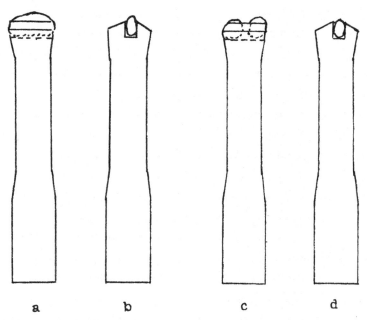

a   b   c   d

Figure 18—DIAMOND DRILLS.
    a and b. Two views of a drill with one diamond.
    c and d. Two views of a drill with two diamonds.

---

diamond is more rugged but cuts more slowly due to its dead center resistance. The drill with the two diamonds cuts faster because the dead center core is broken out of the hole as the drilling progresses instead of having to be worn away, but the drill is quite frail. For holes of about 1/8″ dia. the drill with the single diamond is rugged enough that it can have applied to it sufficient pressure to overcome the dead center resistance. Therefore this type is more suitable for the larger of the drills in the range of sizes from 3/32″ to 3/16″. The smaller drills, being too frail to stand sufficient pressure to overcome the dead center resistance, are better made with two diamonds. It should be kept in mind that the smaller the hole being drilled, the greater is the proportion of its area that is dead center or approaching dead center.

The making of both types of drills is accomplished in the same way. A rod about the size of the finished drill is slotted across the center of its end as shown in Fig. 18. Broken fragments of black diamond are chosen to fit either the whole slot or just less than one half the slot.   The sides of the slot are then squeezed together with pliers to hold the diamond in place temporarily.   They are next firmly seated in place either by peening with a light hammer or by brazing.   When they are well anchored, the drill is chucked in a lathe and the surplus metal projecting past the diamond at the front and on the sides is cut away with a file and also the body of the rod is filed down somewhat to give clearance.

In using these drills several precautions should be taken. The speed may be anything from 500 rpm to 3000 rpm. Probably about 1500 rpm is best.   The drill must be brought down gently against the work.   The required pressure must be learned by experience.   It varies greatly with the individual drill as, when made of rough diamonds, no two will have exactly the same characteristics.   The drill should be operated only with the work submerged in water.   It is unsafe to let the drill break through the back side of a stone.   It will flake the stone and may break the drill.   The hole should be drilled to within about 1/16" of the back of the stone and the stone then turned over and drilled from the back side, thus allowing the holes to meet within the stone.   As they approach the meeting point, the pressure should be lightened.   The drill should be frequently lifted from the work to prevent its getting hot.

The Rod Drill.—Mentioned because it can be and is used for drilling small holes.   Difficult to use and should be avoided by the amateur except as a last resort.   It consists of a rod of brass or steel with a charge of diamond dust.   The method of using it is identical with that of the small tube drill.   Its disadvantage is that it tries to wear away the dead center of the hole, but the stone being harder than the rod, wears a hole in the rod instead.

Fig. 19 shows what happens when this type of drill is being used.   The rod will appear for a while to be cutting.   Then apparently the cutting ceases.   An examination of the hole will show the condition indicated in Fig. 19.   The rod will have cut a groove around its outer edge, but in the center of the hole

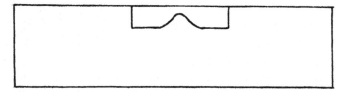

Figure 19.—TYPICAL HOLE MADE WITH ROD DRILL.

will be a pyramid of stone that has not been cut away but that has instead worn a hole in the center of the rod. The remedy is to drive lightly into the hole a new rod of the size of the drill, tapping it gently to break away the pyramid, thereby permitting the rod to cut a little further.

Notes.—No matter what type or size of drill is being used the drill press should be a rugged one with snug fitting spindle. This is especially important on the smaller drills. It should be very sensitive, especially on the smaller drills, so that the amount of pressure can be accurately judged.

Heating will not be excessive on any of the tube drills nor on the rod drill if plenty of kerosene is fed to the work, but the diamond drill, requiring more pressure, will develop dangerous heat unless it is submerged in kerosene.

It is best to drill all holes from both sides, letting them meet within the stone. It is imperative that this be done when the drilling is being done with the diamond drill, because the greater pressure exerted on it will flake the stone when it breaks through. If the material is transparent, it is easy to see how to set the stone for the second part of the hole, so that the holes will meet. With opaque material it is not easy. Another setting job that will give trouble is the setting of beads after they have been rounded so that the hole will be drilled in their center. A simple device will overcome these troubles. When slabs or pendants are to be drilled, they may be cemented to a wood or

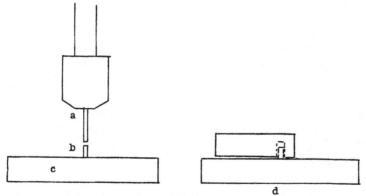

Figure 20.—JIG FOR DRILLING FLATS.
    a. Drill.
    b. Pin.
    c. Metal plate.
    d. Stone installed on plate.

metal block for drilling the first part of the hole. Assuming that this has been done and that the work is ready to be turned over and drilled from the back side, see Fig. 20. Provide a metal plate with a pin the size of the drill projecting from it. The pin is to project from the plate a little less in length than the depth of the hole that has been drilled in the material, so that it does not reach to the bottom of the hole. Lower the drill and adjust the plate to where the drill is directly over the pin. Anchor the plate in this position. Install the stone on the pin with the pin entering the hole that has already been drilled. Fasten the stone in place with cement and proceed to drill until the holes meet.

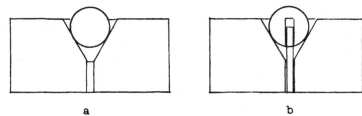

a   b

Figure 21.—JIG FOR DRILLING BEADS. (Section through).
    a. Used for centering first hole.
    b. With pin in place for drilling second hole to meet the first.

The jig for drilling beads is a different form of this same device. See Fig. 21. The block is of metal about 1 1/2″ thick and long enough to afford means of anchoring it to the table of the drill press. A "V" shaped hole is machined in the top of the block, of such size that the beads to be drilled will find a good seat in the hole. From the bottom of the "V" shaped hole a small straight hole, the size of the drill, extends down into or through the block. For the initial drilling the block is anchored on the drill press table so that the center of the hole is directly beneath the drill. The beads are then placed in the hole and are drilled to somewhat more than half way through. When all beads of the lot have had the first part of the holes drilled, a pin is inserted in the small hole at bottom of "V" shaped pit, and allowed to project far enough to enter the bead far enough to determine its position but not far enough to reach the bottom of the drilled hole. (This is to prevent the drill from being injured by striking the pin when the holes meet.)

Any of the drilling methods will leave a rough hole. If the

material is opaque, this is not objectionable. But if the material is transparent, a rough hole through it is unsightly. Also, sometimes the holes do not meet exactly and it is desired to smooth up the point where they meet. Such work can be done with a wire charged with abrasive. Use the fine stranded wire called "picture wire." Use as many strands of it as is desirable. Anchor one end of a piece about two feet long. Feed the wire through the hole to be polished, draw the wire fairly taut and anchor the other end. Daub the wire with paste of Carborundum and water, slide the work back and forth on the wire. The cutting will be quite rapid. Ordinarily No. 600 carbo is suitable for the entire job. If much cutting is to be done, use a coarser grain at the start. If the No. 600 carbo does not leave a sufficiently smooth hole, it can be given a nice polish with pumice paste on the wire.

It is very difficult to get black diamond fragments of the right size and shape to make drills. And black diamonds are required. Bortz has a cleavage so distinct that it splits under the pressure of drilling. Also the making of the drills is a delicate job and only to be learned by practice. It is therefore suggested that the amateur had best buy these drills unless as a matter of pride he prefers to make them and is prepared to waste quite a lot of time and material in learning the trick.

CHAPTER V

BEAD MAKING

Most of the routine of bead making is identical with that cutting cabochon shaped stones. The sawing and rough grinding and polishing have been described in the chapter on cabochon work. The drilling was described in the chapter on Drilling. There remains for discussion here only the matter of getting the beads to the exact shape wanted, either round or cylindrical.

Rough Grinding.—The rough material of which the beads are to be made is sawed first into slabs, then into strips, then into cubes. This sawing should be done carefully so that all cubes are as nearly as possible one size. After the stones are sawed and ground to similar sized cubes, they are held by hand and rough ground on the No. 100 carbo wheel to approximate rounds. This is done by grinding in a systematic manner all 12 edges such equal amounts that the diameters across the newly formed flats are the same as the original diameter of the cubes. Then by visual inspection judge the amounts that should be ground off the corners. This treatment reduces the cube to such a close approximation of a sphere that it will roll in the "bead mill," the use of which is the next step.

Rounding.—The parts for the device herein called a "bead mill" can be made in any foundry and machine shop. Fig. 22 shows a section through this mill which can well be made at home after the castings have been machined. The pan should be about 6″ or 8″ diameter. The groove in its bottom should have a radius somewhat greater than the radius of the largest bead that is to be ground.

To use the mill a set of roughed out beads are placed in the groove. The mill works best if there are enough beads to nearly fill the groove. A charge of carbo paste made with No. 100 carbo and water is put in the pan with the beads. The amount to be used is not critical but should be about a teacup full of the mix. The runner is then brought down against the beads just enough to put the springs under some compression and to cause the pan to float free from its retaining clips. The drill press spindle should be anchored in this position and the press started up. The spindle should not be raised while it is turning but must be left in this position until it has entirely stopped, or else as the runner is lifted, the beads will be thrown out of the groove and perhaps some of them broken. The only attention that

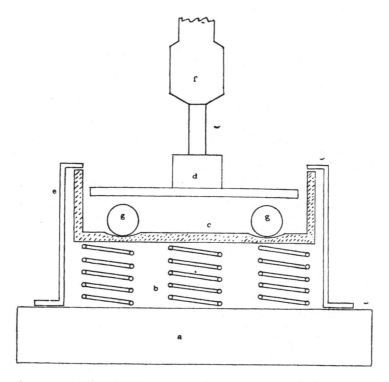

Figure 22.—BEAD MILL.

  a. Wood block.
  b. Nest of from 4 to 6 coiled springs.
  c. Cast iron pan with groove in bottom.
  d. Runner.
  e. Clips to hold pan in place.
  f. Drill press chuck.
  g. Beads in place—only two shown.

---

need be given the operation is to occasionally scrape back into the groove the paste that will have been thrown by centrifugal force to the outer corner of the pan.

In from 15 to 60 minutes, depending on the hardness of the material and the care with which it has been roughed out and the speed of the machine, the beads will be ground to round and will be all the same size. In that sentence is the reason for the statement that the rough grinding should be carefully done. The beads should all be the same size, and in order to get them this way they must all be ground together in the mill until the size is the smallest diameter of the smallest bead.

It is well to start a few more stones through this operation than will actually be wanted, so that if several beads lack a considerable amount of being round when all others are complete, these worst ones may be thrown out rather than all others ground down to their size.

Another point to bear in mind is that if a bead is all true except for one small flat place, this flat place may be used for entering the hole that is to be drilled instead of grinding it further until the last flat disappears.

When all have been rounded, their surface may be improved

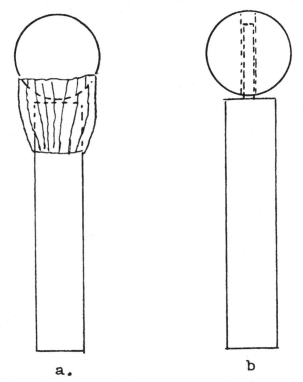

a.   b

Figure 23.—HOLDING BEADS FOR SMOOTHING AND POLISH-
ING.
    a. Attached with cement to a stick.
    b. Held by hand on a pin in the end of a stick.

by doing the same operation over again, using No. 220 carbo. The same mill may be used if the coarser grains are carefully washed out. The mill may run at any speed from 500 to 1000 rpm. It should not run fast enough to cause the pan to dance excessively.

Drilling.—This subject has been covered in a previous chapter.

Smoothing and Polishing.—This is done exactly as similar operations on cabochon shaped stones and has been described in a previous chapter. The stones may be held by either of two methods. See Fig. 23. They may be cemented on a lap stick, or they may be held by hand by the aid of a pin inserted in the end of a hardwood stick. The latter scheme is more convenient and in all respects more suited to the work. The pin should be only a snug fit for the hole in the bead.

Cylindrical Shapes.—Sometimes beads and bracelets are made of long slender cylinders with holes through them lengthwise. When this is wanted, it is suggested that the holes be drilled through the blocks before the blocks are ground down quite to their final size. Then the edges are ground off, holding the

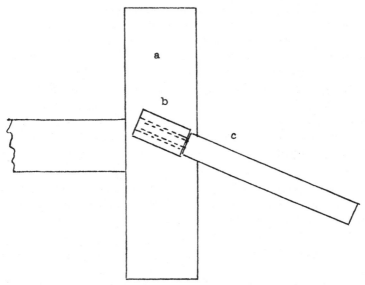

Figure 24.—GRINDING A CYLINDER.
    a. Grinding wheel.
    b. Cylinder being trued.
    c. Stick with pin in end.

cylinder by hand or on a pin in the end of a stick. Then the resulting 8 edges are ground off until the block is roughly cylindrical. The piece may then be ground to a true cylinder by the simple device of installing it on a pin in the end of a hardwood stick and holding it against the abrasive medium at such an angle that the cylinder will be revolved by friction with the abrasive medium but at the same time will present drag enough to result in considerable cutting. See Fig. 24. The grinding medium may be either the periphery of a carbo wheel or the side of a cast iron lap to which carbo paste is applied frequently. The speed at which the cylinder revolves on the pin is controlled by the angle maintained between the stick and the abrasive medium.

Imitation Amber Beads.—Transparent, amber colored bakelite makes beautiful beads and is easy to work. A careful check by the Author showed a total working time of 12 hours for the making of 84 of these beads. The bakelite can be gotten in 1/2″ rods from the Bakelite Corporation. The general scheme of making is the same as for the stone beads but with certain modifications.

The steps in the making are as follows:

Saw the rod into lengths exactly the same as the diameter of the rod. Use a jig for this to insure equal and correct lengths and also to insure squareness of cuts.

Center mark the blanks with a jig and drill holes through the cylinders lengthwise. Better do the job on a drill press if one is available. Use about No. 54 wire drill or equivalent size. This drill is quite frail on account of its size. For that reason let it project from the chuck only far enough to reach through the bead.

Grind off the edges of the ends of the cylinders until they are approximately spherical. Use a No. 100 carbo wheel running wet. Hold the blanks with a tool such as has been illustrated, consisting of a pin in the end of a stick.

Place the blanks in the bead mill with a charge of No. 100 carbo paste. The use of the mill has already been described. The time for this operation will vary from 10 to 15 minutes per batch.

Wash the rounds and the mill; put in a charge of No. FF paste and treat each batch about 5 minutes to further smooth them.

The next job is to smooth the beads with fine pumice powder on a lap of wool carpet or soft felt on the side of a wood wheel. This operation is a fast one; watch it carefully at first or you may get flats. Time required for each bead from 1 1/2 to 2 minutes depending on the skill exercised in manipulating the bead at a uniform and correct speed.

Then polish with tin oxide paste on a lap of wool carpet or soft felt or yielding cloth on the side of a wood wheel. This operation is also a fast one. Time required about the same as for the smoothing.

A further step that can be taken if absolute perfection is sought, is to finish the beads on the periphery of an unsewed cloth lap with tin oxide. This step is not at all necessary.

As the bakelite is very soft it may be scored around the hole if allowed to turn on the pin while riding against the stick. Cut a small leather washer to fit snugly over the pin and against the stick.

It is well to keep the batches separate until after they have had their second cutting in the mill. The different batches will not be of exactly the same size, and if they are mixed during the second cutting, the larger ones will take all the smoothing and the smaller ones be unaffected.

CHAPTER VI

CUTTING FACETED GEMS

General Discussion

As has been mentioned in previous chapters, opaque or translucent gem material is usually cut with a knob shaped curved surface crown, this shape being known as "en cabochon" usually shortened to "cabochon."

Transparent gems are usually cut with their surfaces bounded by flat faces, symmetrically arranged. These gems are called "faceted."

The cutting of this form presents problems that are distinct from any met with in cabochon cutting, but in general they need not be more serious nor difficult of solution than the problems faced by the beginner in working the simpler cabochon shapes. Note the term "in general." Many specific problems will arise. Some of these will seem almost impossible of solution. The amateur may never find the answer to some of them. But they are specific and limited and need not interfere with the amateur's enjoyment of this fascinating branch of the work. For example, one should not lose sleep because he cannot polish a large transparent opal with facets and have no scratches on it. There are two alternatives: one can either let the opal alone and be happy in the knowledge that there are a dozen kinds of stone which he can polish without scratches, or he can polish it as best he can, leaving on it such scratches as he cannot remove, and be agreeably conscious of the fact that with all its scratches, he has an entirely presentable gem which, to the casual observer, will appear to be perfect. In other words, this plea is not to take faceting too seriously in the beginning. But, in the beginning, be content to take up basic considerations only "and all these things shall be added unto you." Problems of cutting, aligning, cementing, and polishing will not be solved in a day. Nor will they all be solved in any one lifetime. But almost "in a day" the beginner can produce gems of which he may be justly proud and which will give him as great a thrill as he will ever experience from the cutting of later, more perfectly fashioned stones. Keep in mind that professional cutters have spent years learning to do perfectly what you are now attempting, and in the beginning be content, if necessary, with gems somewhat short of perfect.

There are two ways to hold gems for cutting and polishing to the shape wanted. One way is to cement them onto a lap stick and hold them by hand only, against the lap, having as a general guide, the "gem peg." This device is an approximate cylinder anchored in place above the face of the lap. It has many notches in its side. The tail end of the lap stick rests in one of the notches, giving the worker a firm rest for the lap stick and also acting as a guide to position of the gem on the lap. This scheme is widely used by professional cutters. It is used practically not at all by amateurs, as its use requires much practice and skill.

The amateur invariably uses an indexing device to hold the gem in position. These are all essentially the same but differ in many details and in their adaptation to either a vertical or a horizontal lap. This is no place to enter into a discussion of the merits of each type. But in order to be specific instead of general, it is necessary to choose one type or the other and to consider the chosen one to the exclusion of the other. Because the Author has always used the vertical lap, he will describe that type here and will use it in this demonstration of gem cutting. This choice must not be construed as an argument against the horizontal form of lap.

Preliminary Work.—It is generally the case that one who begins faceting has been doing cabochon work. When this is true, he already has in his shop all the necessary equipment for doing the "preliminary work" which consists only of sawing the material to size and roughing it to shape. The matter of roughing deserves a little consideration. Such details as the proper orientation of the gem to the crystal (where such considerations enter the picture) will be taken up later. At present we are concerned only with the mechanical features of easily and properly getting the block of gem material into such shape that a minimum of work will be necessary on the slower cutting later operation.

We are going to deal for the present only with the round brilliant as shown in Fig. 30. The terms that are ordinarily used in describing parts of the gem are:

The Table—The large flat surface on the top of the gem.

The Culet—The small flat surface at the rear of the gem. Usually omitted on all stones except the diamond.

The Girdle—The widest part of the gem.

The Pavillion—The part of the gem below the girdle.

The Crown—The part of the gem above the girdle.

The Author usually thinks of the "crown" and the "pavillion" of a gem as the "front" and the "rear" and will generally use these terms.

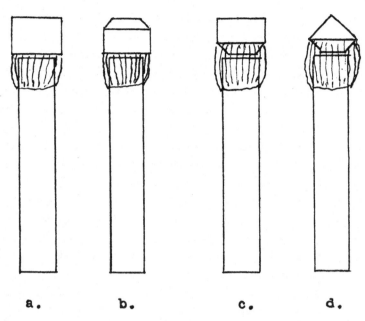

a.   b.   c.   d.

Figure 25.—STEPS IN ROUGHING OUT A ROUND BRILLIANT.

The gem material is first sawed to a cube. Its height from culet to table should be about 3/4 its width across the girdle. The cube should be cemented on a lap stick as shown in Fig. 25, with the large dimension at right angles to the stick. With this setting the cube is to be ground to a cylinder and one end of the cylinder is to be beveled at an angle of about 45° to the girdle, the bevel extending 1/3 of the distance from the top end of the cylinder. See Fig. 25. Then reverse the stone as at "c" and grind the other end of the cylinder to a point, letting this new bevel just meet the old one as at "d" in the same figure. The angle is again about 45° and "d" shows the appearance of the completely roughed out gem.

It may be mentioned here that when other shapes are to be cut, they should be cemented on a stick for roughing, as this scheme gives the worker better control of the cutting, and the resulting roughed gem will be more nearly the desired shape than if it is held by hand only.

Equipment

1. Faceting device. Some form of tool which will enable the user to present to the lap, with certainty of correctness, the area of a gem on which grinding or polishing is to be done. This tool may take any of many different forms, but some such device is a necessity. In order to make the instruction clear and definite there is included here a description of the tool used by the Author. See Fig. 26. The parts are:

A 12″ square cast iron bedplate carrying a 90° slotted sector graduated in degrees.

A standrod arm, pivoted on this base and arranged to be tightened in position at any point of its travel and with a pointer so that its position on the graduated sector may be noted and recorded.

A standrod carrying a crosshead free to slide on the rod.

An index wheel sector attached to the crosshead by means of a screw through a slot in the crosshead. This screw is on the

Figure 26.—FACETING TOOL.

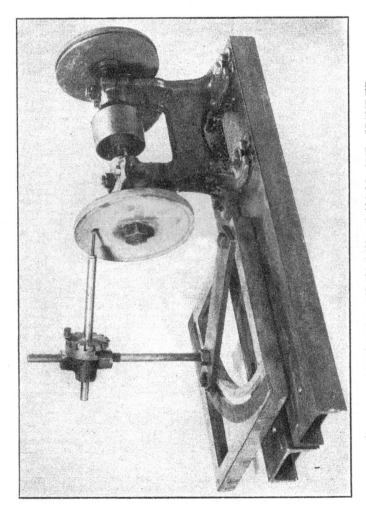

Figure 27.—ASSEMBLY OF FACETING TOOL AND GRINDER.

far side of the crosshead as it appears in Fig. 27. (The assembly of this tool with the lap, Fig. 27, shows the opposite side of the crosshead and the method of fastening.) This sector should have a graduated section extending over the spread of two slots on the index wheel, with a heavy central mark to match a mark on the crosshead. This is to enable one to keep the sector set in "normal" position and, on occasion, to skew it a determined amount and to be able to record the amount of skew.

A lap stick, turned from brass integral with the index wheel which appears in the picture as a slotted disc. The tail end of this lap stick passes through a horizontal hole in the crosshead and through a corresponding hole in the index wheel sector.

An index wheel, just mentioned as being made integral with the lap stick. It has 16 slots equidistant, numbered consecutively from 1 to 16. These slots are just wide enough to admit a screw which passes through them and into a tapped hole in the index wheel sector.

Several lap stick points. Made of screws with heads projecting. These points are locked with a nut into a hole tapped in the end of the lap stick.

It is desirable but not essential that the length of the lap stick and its point from the standrod be the same as the length of the standrod arm from its pivoted point to the standrod.

The assembly of the tool with the grinding head is shown in Fig. 27. The pivoted point of the standrod arm should be directly beneath the center of the face of the lap.

The operation of the tool is briefly:

The end of the lap stick point is flattened with a file or grinding wheel. The gem is attached to the lap stick with cement. Cutting may then proceed.

A protractor square is used to set the lap stick at the correct angle with the lap to produce the desired inclination of facets to girdle. The 16 main positions of an ordinary round brilliant are determined by the 16 slots in the index wheel. Skew facets are obtained by moving the index wheel sector a correct amount, then proceeding, with the sector locked in its new position, to cut all corresponding skew facets with regular settings in the slots of the index wheel. The work will be described in detail later.

Keep in mind that any tool used must be universally adjustable through 360° around the girdle and through 90° around the axis of the gem.

2. An iron lap. Plain cast iron machined true all over. Suggested size 6" x 3/4" thick. For cutting.

3. A pure tin lap. Machined true all over. Same size and thickness as the iron lap. For polishing.

4. No. 600 Carborundum powder for cutting.

5. Tin oxide for polishing.

6. Damascus Ruby Powder for polishing a few of the special gems such as topaz and zircon.

7. Extra hard chasers cement for cementing the gem to the lap stick.

8. Stick shellac. For attaching the table of the gem to the table of the lap stick point. The chasers cement has so much body that if it is used for this purpose, it is hard to get the gem to a true seat.

9. Some form of jig for setting the gem correctly on the lap stick. The axis of the gem must be parallel to the axis of the lap stick; otherwise the gem will be cut "lopsided." It is desirable that the axis of the gem positively coincide with the axis of the lap stick, but this is not essential. The Author makes no provision in his jig for centering the gem on the lapstick point but does this by eye and finds it close enough for practical purposes. A suitable jig is shown in Fig. 28.

At this point it might be well to note that some cutters use a bronze lap instead of the iron one for cutting. If bronze is used, the same abrasive, No. 600 carbo, is suitable. Other cutters use lead for cutting all stones of ordinary hardness. If lead is used, the abrasive should be No. FF carbo.

This is also as good time as any to go into the matter of conditioning the tin lap. A smooth lap will not polish a gem

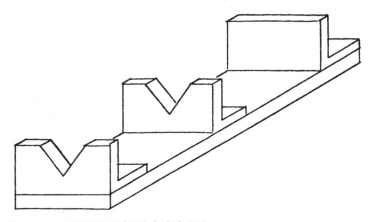

Figure 28.—CRADLE TYPE OF JIG.
For setting gem on lapstick.

but is sure to cause scratches. These scratches are called "grain marks" and are probably caused by the abrasive and the cut away gem material forming compact large grains which roll between the gem and the lap, gouging a row of holes in the gem if the gem is in close contact with the lap, as is the case if the lap is smooth. The remedy for this trouble is to thoroughly score the lap as shown in Fig. 29. This scoring is done with a knife, spacing the marks about 1/4" apart at the periphery of the lap. After the scores have been cut, the lap is put on the machine and the machine is started up, having it revolve in the same direction it will have when used for polishing. Daub on its face a thick paste of tin oxide and water. Then proceed to smooth the lap partially by holding against it a flat piece of agate or quartz about 3/4" diameter. The purpose of this treatment is to smooth the tops of the ridges made by the knife cuts to narrow flat tables. This treatment should be continued several

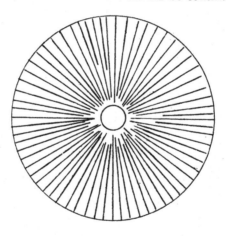

a.

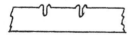

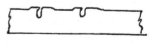

b.   c.

Figure 29.—THE SCORED TIN LAP.
    a. Plan of scoring.
    b. Enlarged section of face of lap showing knife marks.
    c. Enlarged section of face of lap after tops of ridges have been smoothed down by friction with large piece of agate or quartz.

minutes and should be concluded with a brief period of polishing with the lap dry.

Cutting a Round Brilliant

The initial attempt should be a round brilliant. It should be about 1/4″ diameter. Rock crystal is cheap, abundant, and suitable for this work. The worker should first get fixed in his mind as firmly as possible what constitutes a standard round brilliant and what cuts are necessary to produce it. The first work will be the standard brilliant, except that where skew facets are shown in the standard brilliant, the "intermediate" facets of this stone will not be sewed. (The index device has 16 regular fixed positions. A skew facet is one that cannot be produced with any of these regular settings but for the production of which the whole index head must be "skewed").

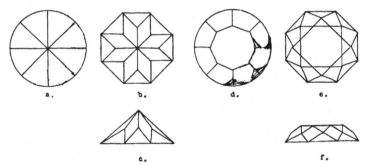

Figure 30.—STEPS IN CUTTING MODIFIED ROUND BRIL-
LIANT.
   a. Plan of rear of gem showing main facets only.
   b. Plan of rear of gem with all facets cut.
   c. Elevation of rear of gem with all facets cut.
   d. Plan of front of gem with main facets only.
   e. Plan of front of gem with all facets cut.
   f. Elevation of front of gem with all facets cut.

To get a picture of the steps used in producing this "modified brilliant" see Fig. 30. "a" is a plan of the rear of the gem after the eight main facets only have been cut. .The settings for these cuts are the odd numbers on the index wheel. "b" is the plan after all rear facets have been cut, etc.

The stone has already been roughed out as shown in Fig. 25. It is first to be stuck onto the lap stick point and have its table leveled and polished. Set the faceting tool in such a position that the lap stick makes an angle of about 20° with the face of the lap. Put the cast iron lap on the machine. Holding the lap stick point and a piece of hard chasers cement in the flame of an alcohol lamp, build up quite a "wad" of cement on the point. Grasp the roughed out gem with pliers or tweezers with the sharp point of the rear projecting. Hold the gem and the cement in the flame and thoroughly coat the rear of the gem with the cement. Laying aside the piece of cement, hold the gem and the cement covered lap stick point at the same time in the flame. When both are sufficiently warm, stick the rear point of the gem into the side of the wad of cement on the lap stick point. With the fingers wet, mould the cement around the gem up to but not beyond the girdle. While the cement is still warm, swing the gem against the lap so that the table bears truly and firmly against the lap, and hold it in this position until the cement hardens.

The table is now ready to be cut. Start up the machine, having the lap revolve in such direction that the gem drags on the lap. (As in Fig. 27 the lap should revolve clockwise when looking toward the machine.) The speed should be about 400 rpm. Daub on the lap a paste of No. 600 carbo and water and proceed to cut the table until, when looked at with magnifier, it is apparent that all parts of the table have been cut by this operation and that there are no low edges. When the cutting has just begun, it is well to examine the stone to be sure that it is properly set and that the cutting is in the right place. If the setting is not correct, it may be easily adjusted by swinging the standrod arm or the index wheel sector or both until the table is parallel to the lap.

When the table has been cut true, the cutting lap is removed, the arbor nut washed, the gem and the cement washed with a stiff brush in warm water, and the hands of the worker washed and dried. The tin polishing lap is now put in place. Be sure that it has been conditioned as previously described. Apply to the tin lap a very thin mix of tin oxide and water. One teaspoonful of tin oxide in 1/4 pint of water is thick enough. The mix should be applied sparingly with the tip of a finger. It is well to remember that more scratching is caused by an excessive amount of abrasive than by all other causes combined.

Proceed to polish. This should be done by moderate pressure for short periods of from 15 to 30 seconds, applying to the lap at each interruption a small amount of the tin oxide paste. When the surface appears to the naked eye to be completely polished, it will often be found that there are several or many fine scratches visible with the aid of the magnifier. From this condition the perfect polish should be gotten by polishing on a strictly dry lap. Apply the usual touch of tin oxide and allow it to become wholly dry before touching the stone to the lap. The pressure is still moderate to light. The gem must be watched carefully to prevent its getting too hot. If too much heat develops, it may crack the gem and it will certainly cause it to come loose in the cement.

The next operation is to recement the stone to the lap stick in a new position and to cut the rear facets. The gem is warmed and removed from the cement and the cement scraped off it. The excess cement may be removed from the lap stick point and this same point used for the new job, or, better, the old point should be laid aside in reserve for later similar jobs and a new one used for this work. The several points should be of varying shapes and sizes. All should be flat on the end. There should be several round ones of different sizes and a few oblong rectangular and oval shaped ones. Choose for this work a round point having a diameter about the same as that of the table of the gem. Warm the point and hard chasers cement and bank the cement around the point but not on the flat face of the point. While the point is still warm, wipe a stick of shellac, warmed, across the flat face, leaving a film of shellac on the face. Grasp the gem with tweezers or pliers, warm it and wipe the stick shellac across its table. Then, warming the gem and the lap stick point at the same time, press them together, the gem table firmly against the flat end of the point. Lay the lapstick in he cradle jig shown in Fig. 28, with the point of the rear of the gem pressed firmly against the table of the jig. Keeping the cement warm by occasionally holding it for short periods in the flame, work the cement, with the wet fingers, in a solid bank around and against the gem up to but not beyond the girdle.

The gem is now ready for the cutting of the rear facets. For quartz these rear main facets are to be inclined 41° from the girdle. The measurement of this inclination must be made by measuring the angle of the lap stick with the lap. It must be kept in mind that the angle made by the lap stick with the lap is the complement of the angle of the facet to the girdle. So that now when an angle of 41° is wanted between the facet and the girdle, the lap stick must be set at an angle of 49° with the lap. The setting of the lap stick angle must be determined by use of a protractor square. No machine can properly do this, due to the fact that this angle is changed by either of three variable factors: the position of the tool relative to the lap (thickness of lap), length of lap stick point, size and shape of gem. So, with a protractor square, set the lap stick at an angle of 49° with the lap. Make a record of the position of the standrod arm on the base sector, as this setting must be used later for polishing.

Proceed to cut the eight main rear facets. Set index wheel in position 1. Grind with the No. 600 carbo paste on the iron lap until this facet appears to be cut a sufficient amount. Now, do not move to position 3 to cut the adjacent facet as might seem logical, but move to position 9 and cut the opposite facet. Visual inspection must be relied on to determine the amount of cutting to be done on each facet. Then move to position 13, then to position 5. The stone will then be a four sided pyramid. Then move two positions in either direction and cut off a corner of the four sided pyramid. Then by steps of four positions cut off the three remaining corners. The faces will now appear as in Fig. 30 a. Note that notches with odd numbers have been used for these main facets.

Shift the index wheel one position only, to any even number. Swing the index head about 5° toward the lap and proceed to cut the eight intermediate "girdle facets." The extent of cutting on each is to be judged by eye. They should just touch each other at the girdle or should slightly overlap, thereby producing between them a short straight line parallel to the axis of the gem. At this stage the gem is like "b" and "c" Fig. 30.

Remove the iron lap, wash the gem and cement with a stiff brush in warm water, wash and dry the hands. Place the tin lap in position and polish all rear facets. The same notes as to polishing apply as were given for polishing the table. It is best to polish the girdle facets first and then the main facets. This saves one setting of the tool and also allows the larger main facets to be polished away from polished edges instead of from unpolished edges, which is a distinct advantage.

This polishing having been completed, the gem is warmed and removed from the cement and the surplus cement scraped off it. The wad of cement on the lap stick point is now warmed and with wet fingers a portion of it is worked around in front of the end of the point where it is formed into a cylinder about the diameter of the gem. The gem is now warmed and the newly cut rear of it is daubed with hot cement. Then the gem and the wad of cement are warmed at the same time and the rear of the gem is pressed into the cement. The lap stick is then laid in the cradle jig with the table of the gem pressed against the table of the jig and the cement formed close around the gem with wet fingers. It is held in this position until the cement hardens.

The front main facets are to be cut at an angle of 45° with the girdle. The lap stick setting with the lap is then the complement of 45° which is 45°.

The eight front main facets are then cut, using the same sequence of settings as was used on the rear main facets and judging by eye when each is sufficiently cut. The crown now appears as at "d" Fig. 30. (Again the odd numbers were used for the main facets, the even numbers for the intermediate ones.) Shift the index head one position to any even number. Move the standrod arm about 15° away from the lap and cut the small triangular facets at the table. These should just meet at the edge of the table, and the points of them should extend nearly half way to the girdle. The exact setting of the standrod arm is to be adjusted by cut and try to give these proportions. These facets should be cut consecutively around the gem and each compared carefully with the preceding one for size.

When these eight table facets have been cut, the standrod arm is shifted to about 5° nearer to the lap than was the setting for the main facets. The girdle facets are now to be cut. The exact setting is adjusted by cut and try to where these facets will just meet at the girdle, or overlap slightly, while the upper point of each just meets the lower point of the table facets. When these have all been cut, the iron lap is removed, the gem washed as previously described, the tin lap is put in place, and the front facets are polished. The order in which this is done is not material. The Author finds it convenient to polish them in reverse order to that in which they were cut: viz., polish first the girdle facets, then the table facets, then the main ones.

The gem is then warmed with the lamp, removed from the cement, immersed for a short while in acetone or for a longer time in alcohol to soften the cement, washed carefully in the soaking medium, and dried with a soft cloth, which must be free of lint.

The matter of inclination of facets for other gem stones will be touched on in a later chapter on Optics.

The Standard Round Brilliant.—It was noted that the stone just described was a modified cut. It was used to allow the beginner to get some practice in cutting and polishing without being too much hampered by complications of settings. It avoided all skew facets.

The only difference between the gem just described and the standard round brilliant is that where the modified cut used 8 triangular facets at the girdle, both front and rear, the standard cut uses 16 triangular facets on both front and rear. These are gotten by splitting each of the 8 into two equal triangles by skewing the index head. See Fig. 31, for the appearance of these skew facets. The setting for cutting these is simple on the tool used herein. When the tool has been set in position to cut the

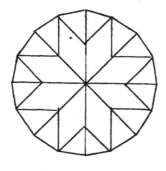

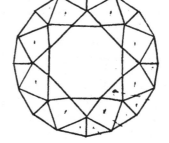

Plan. Plan.

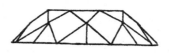

Elevation. **Elevation.**

Rear of Gem, Front of Gem.

Figure 31.—STANDARD ROUND BRILLIANT CUT.

girdle facets as in the modified cut, the screw holding the index wheel sector in place against the crosshead is loosened, and the index wheel sector is skewed a proper amount to one side of the normal setting. Then, using the regular positions on the index wheel, eight of these facets are cut. The sector is then turned an equal amount in the opposite direction from normal and the other 8 facets are cut. There is no way except by cut and try to determine what settings to use. The shape of the facet may be changed either by varying the inclination of it to the girdle or by changing the amount of skew. The adjustment varies with the height of gem compared to its spread and must be separately determined for each gem.

Other Shapes.—No discussion will be given of other shapes. Other shapes are shown in Fig. 32. After the user becomes sufficiently familiar with the faceting tool, he will find that it is actually a "tool," a device with which he can get any result he wishes. The initial feeling of bewilderment at its necessary settings quickly passes and one handles the tool almost instinctively.

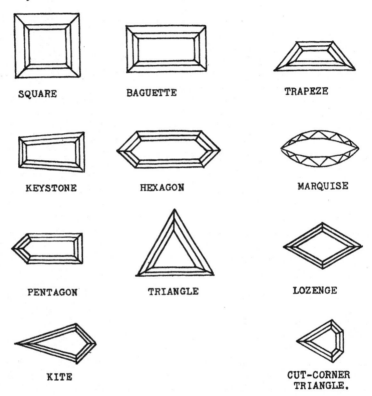

SQUARE   BAGUETTE   TRAPEZE

KEYSTONE   HEXAGON   MARQUISE

PENTAGON   TRIANGLE   LOZENGE

KITE   CUT-CORNER
                                  TRIANGLE.

Figure 32.—SOME OF THE SHAPES COMMONLY USED IN CUTTING FACETED GEMS.

Stones Requiring Special Treatment

Topaz.—Topaz has a weak structure along the cleavage plane. With standard treatment with tin oxide, wet, it is impossible to get even a fair degree of polish.

The gem should be properly oriented in the crystal. The cleavage is at right angles to the axis of the crystal. The gem should be so roughed from the crystal that no facet will be parallel to the cleavage plane. This condition may be met by cutting with gem axis declined about either 10° or 100° from the axis of the crystal.

The gem is cut with the standard procedure outlined for the ordinary run of gems.

The polishing is done with Damascus Ruby Powder, nearly or wholly dry. The lap condition is to be the same as in standard practice. If it seems best to polish entirely dry (as is usually the case), the ruby powder may be applied to the lap by having a thin film of it scattered on the bottom of a shallow vessel and occasionally pressing the tip of the forefinger into this film of powder, and touching it to the revolving lap. The stone heats very rapidly under this treatment; so work periods must be very short, the actual periods depending on pressure being applied but probably not in excess of 5 seconds. It is well to occasionally wash the lap to free it of debris, then let it entirely dry before proceeding.

Zircon.—The notes given for topaz as to orientation of the gem do not apply to zircon, but the details of polishing are the same.

Olivine (Peridot).—Notes in general the same as for zircon except cut with No. 600 carbo on lead. Grains as coarse as No. FF may be used if desired. Olivine is more "tender" than either topaz or zircon. Tin oxide will polish it but is slower than ruby powder. Should be polished entirely dry. The speed should be rather low, from 200 to 400 rpm, and the pressure very light. The lap must be more nearly smooth than with almost any other gem and the abrasive applied very sparingly. In short, it must be handled very "gently."

Kunzite.—Has perfect cleavage and weak structure. The gem must be oriented with its table at right angles to the axis of the crystal.

The chief trouble that will be experienced is the tendency for the gem to split on a weak cleavage plane. While this will happen occasionally, no matter how carefully the gem is handled, it is often due to too rough handling in either sawing or roughing out. The damage may not show up at the time it is inflicted, but the gem may be weakened and under the heat of polishing may actually part on a weakened cleavage plane. The following precautions will help to control this trouble:

Saw only with a truly round saw to eliminate shocks. A well trued diamond saw is best for this work.

Rough out on a fine grained carbo wheel (No. FF is good) that has just been trued and has no flats on it. Use only light pressure. Grind only parallel to the axis of the crystal. The object still being to avoid shocks to the gem. The reason for using the fine wheel is two-fold. Shocks will be less harsh. Also, grains of carbo sometimes stick into the gem and act as wedges, causing it to split. The finer the grains the less is this danger.

Cut on a lead lap. Carbo as coarse as No. 220 may be used for this, but the Author's preference is for No. 600, even though it is very slow when used on lead.

Polish with tin oxide. All operations must be done carefully.

Corundum.—This material with a hardness of 9 takes a treatment entirely different from any of those so far outlined. Commercial cutting of corundum is usually done with a diamond charged copper lap. As few amateurs will care to invest in this device for the small amount of cutting they are likely to do on this particular material, the procedure as outlined will neglect this device and make it possible for the amateur to cut these gems with no special equipment except a copper lap for polishing.

The gem is roughed out on the No. 100 carbo wheel. The process is slow and cuts the wheel at a rapid rate. If one wishes to sacrifice some time to save some wear on carbo wheel, the gem may be roughed out on an iron lap with a paste of No. 100 carbo. Use thick paste and heavy pressure.

The cutting is done on the cast iron lap with paste of No. 150 or No. FF carbo or No. 500 Norbide. No particular notes regarding the cutting except that it is slow. Corundum is peculiar in that it is so very varying in hardness. Each gem will have in it both hard and soft spots. These show up clearly in the cutting. The hard spots are highly resistant to Carborundum and while one of three of these will hold up the cutting on a particular facet, the soft spots on the same facet are being undercut. The trouble will persist through the polishing process, often giving to certain facets an etched appearance that the Author has never been able to control. It should be kept in mind that an entire facet may consist of soft material. Therefore it is well to examine each facet very promptly after cutting has begun. If the facet happens to be all soft, it may be overcut in 1/10 the time that was required to cut another similar facet.

A method alternate to the above and that is very effective is to do the cutting on a diamond charged lap. Take a copper disc of hard rolled copper, about 4" or 5" in dia. x 1/4" thick and charge it with diamond dust. Score the lap as is done for polishing, by rubbing a piece of coarse Carborundum radially over all the surface. Mix a carat of No. 1 diamond dust with about 20 drops of olive oil. Smear this thoroughly over a band about 1" wide on the disc. Rub this dust into the lap with a piece of agate flatted on one side, with strokes at right angles to the scoring. The agate should be about 1/2" square with the edges of its flat surface rounded. Continue this rubbing until the surface has a dry appearance with no oil apparent.

In use, after each application of the stone wipe the lap with a brush or cloth wet with kerosene.

A finer diamond dust will cut slower but will leave less polishing to be done.

The polishing is done with a paste of either tripoli or rotten stone on a copper lap. This lap should be scored as was specified for the tin lap. The paste may be applied rather heavily at first, but the finishing should be done with a very thin paste. In fact it probably pays to have two mixes of paste, one thick for the beginning of the polish and one thin for the latter part of it.

An alternate to the above polishing method is the use of Carborundum Buffing Powder, Grade A No. 1 Fine, instead of tripoli or rottenstone. Users have reported it very superior and much faster.

A word should be said as to care in roughing out sapphire. The color in sapphire is usually unevenly distributed. It often happens that a sapphire with apparently good color will actually have one small spot of color and the rest of the gem be either colorless or of some pale color other than blue. Therefore the rough should be examined carefully before shaping progresses too far. If the color is in one spot or if the color is more intense in one spot than in another, this spot should be made the culet of the gem. In this way the color will appear to be evenly distributed through the completed gem.

Sometimes a crystal will have a spot of good color so located that it cannot possibly be incorporated in any gem that may be cut from the piece. Each crystal deserves study before cutting.

Spinel.—Usually works beautifully, but occasionally a difficult stone will be found. The Author does not know the reason for this. Spinel is treated exactly like topaz except that it is not necessary to orient the gem in the crystal.

Synthetic Corundum.—Treat as natural corundum.

Synthetic Spinel.—Treat as natural spinel.

General Notes

The procedure that was outlined just before taking up the matter of "gems requiring special treatment" might well be called "standard practice;" so, in the later notes it has been referred to as such. It is applicable to nearly all gems. The chief exceptions have been noted. The purpose of these general notes is to call attention to certain points which if introduced into the routine descriptions might only be confusing.

Assuming that the bench grinder shaft is level, it is very necessary that the standrod arm be plumb in all positions. To insure this it is well to mount the grinding head and the faceting tool on a common iron or steel base. The tool can then be shimmed until it has the correct position. This is not of great importance in cutting round brilliants, especially of the smaller sizes, but it is highly important if long narrow facets are to be cut.

The cement used for setting gems on the lap stick for facet cutting should be chosen with care. It should have "tackiness" and strength and a high melting point. Many formulae are used, but the Author has found Dixon's Fig. 20343 Extra Hard Chasers Cement most satisfactory.

Loose coarse abrasive is not likely to become embedded in the tin lap. But it does happen sometimes. It can usually be removed by scraping the surface with a razor blade while the lap is running.

Care should be taken to get the main facets the same size. The "measuring" must be done by eye. It is hard to look at two facets side by side and correctly judge their relative width. In the case of the rear main facets, they may be judged with fair accuracy by observing the rear of the stone in plan, and seeing that each line separating two facets passes directly through the point of the gem and matches exactly a corresponding line on the other side of the point. This means of inspecting is especially valuable in getting the first 4 sides of the pyramid cut to equal widths. The widths of the front main facets may best be judged by inspection of the length of the line where each joins the polished table. This will be found more accurate than observing the stone in side elevation. It is the main facets that require special attention, as, if they are equal in size, the intermediate facets will almost automatically be of equal size, but if the main ones are not of equal size, the intermediate ones cannot be so.

Be careful to keep carbo grains out of the crosshead bearings. While loose crosshead bearings are not a serious trouble when small round brilliants are being cut, they make it impossible to do accurate work where long rectangular facets are involved. It is well to make the faceting tool with removable bearings in the crosshead and to change these when the wear becomes excessive.

The Author does not know how to insure the cutting of true flat facets with the carbo paste. When the gem is applied to a lap charged with the loose paste, it may be maneuvered in either of three ways. It may be held in one position on the lap. If this is done the facet is quite sure to be cut in grooves. It may be applied out near the periphery of the lap and moved gradually toward the center. In this case it will usually be cut faster on the edge of the facet next to the arbor. It may be applied near the arbor and moved slowly toward the periphery. Observation of the Author has not been extensive enough to show conclusively the behavior due to this movement, but apparently it gives no better results than movements in the opposite direction. The shape of a facet and the angle at which its leading edge contacts the lap is also a factor in uneven cutting. If the leading edge of a facet lies on other than a radial line on the lap, it appears that the abrasive is scraped from the lap by the part of the edge that lies forward in the travel, and is concentrated on the lagging part of the edge, thereby causing overcutting on that part of the facet directly behind this lagging edge against which the abrasive was "piled up." Definitely, such uneven cutting is at a minimum when the paste is thin, though thin paste also makes for slower cutting.

Scratches.—Every beginner will inevitably have trouble with scratches. His normal reaction is to look for contamination by coarse abrasives. These scratches will not be calculable nor predictable except in one respect. They will almost invariably show up when, and only when, the polish is closely approaching the perfect condition. The Author does not know the reason for this but believes it has to do with intimacy of contact. In other respects this scratching appears to follow no rules. It will not be of any set size or pattern or location on the facet. Sometimes it will constitute a deep furrow all the way across the facet. Or it may originate on the leading edge and die within the facet, or it may originate on the face and extend to the trailing edge, or it may originate and die on the facet without touching any edge. If the scratch appears to be a deep furrow with apparently smooth and sloping sides, it may be caused by a peculiar structure on the leading edge of the facet. There may be a slight irregularity on the leading edge that acts as a funnel, scraping the abrasive from areas on one or both sides of the furrow and concentrating it at one point to produce the furrow. This condition may usually be corrected by scraping the edge of the facet where the trouble is occurring, with a knife, or by rubbing it with a piece of fine sandpaper to destroy the funnel effect.

If the scratches are rough or irregular and there are several or many of them, and they extend all the way across the facet, a contamination is indicated. The lap should be washed and scraped with a razor blade while running, then washed again. This treatment will almost invariably clear the lap. If there is danger that the coarse abrasive is in the mix, the mix should of course be abandoned and the vessel washed.

If the scratches are irregular, or if they are smooth in appearance but do not extend all the way across the facet, they are almost certain to be "grain marks." The grain mark is caused apparently by many fine particles of abrasive and probably of cut away gem material becoming compacted into a large irregular shaped "grain" and being "tumbled," under pressure, between the lap and the gem. In this tumbling its sharp points gouge out a series of holes in the gem. It will probably break down under the pressure into its original fine particles but not until the damage has been done.

Naturally it is more troublesome on soft stones than on hard ones. On very soft stones such as opal, the Author has found it almost impossible to control it. But certain practices will tend to minimize the trouble:

1. The lap must be conditioned as already pointed out. Presumably the reason for the effectiveness of this treatment is, that with the lap in "hills and hollows" the loose abrasive and the cut-away gem material will fall harmlessly into the low places where they cannot become compacted by pressure and where the gem rides above them.

2. The abrasive paste must be very thin. A teaspoonful of paste to 1/4 pint of water is thick enough. If a small amount of pure soap is added to the mix, it will help to hold the abrasive in suspension and to keep it of correct consistency for a much longer time. "Gardinal," a synthetic soap, made by the National Aniline and Chemical Co., is excellent for the purpose.

3. The required degree of roughness of lap to give best results on a given gem cannot be predetermined. It varies considerably. In general, for a particular kind of material, the larger the facet, the coarser should be the scoring. It will sometimes be found that if a lap is in perfect condition for polishing a facet of medium size, it is too smooth for a large facet and too rough for a small one. When the lap is too rough for a small facet, the polishing should be concentrated on a narrow streak on the lap, and this narrow streak will soon be pressed down to requisite smoothness. If the lap is too smooth

for a particular facet, it may be sufficiently roughened by hard rubbing with coarse sandpaper.

4. Again, in general, neglecting certain weaknesses of structure inherent in certain gems, the softer the gem the more susceptible it is to grain marks. Combating these troubles in very soft gems such as opal often seems to be hopeless. A fairly effective aid is to do all polishing on a strictly dry lap. Or if the facet is a large one such as a table, the polish may be begun wet and changed to dry at the point where experience shows scratching is likely to begin.

In determining which of several possible schemes are to be used for charging the lap, the liability to cause scratching should be taken into consideration. The several schemes possible are outlined in the order of their liability to cause scratching:

(a) Paste applied and used wet.

(b) Paste applied wet, partially rubbed off with cloth but used while lap still wet.

(c) Abrasive applied wet but allowed to dry before using.

(d) Abrasive applied dry and used without wiping off any of that applied.

(e) Abrasive applied dry and wiped off with cloth before using.

(f) Abrasive applied dry or wet, then washed off with wet cloth with lap running, and lap allowed to completely dry before gem applied to it.

Needless to say, the last named method leaves little of the abrasive on the lap, but it leaves enough to be quite effective on very soft stones and will often control scratching when all other means have failed.

5. Speed sometimes has something to do with liability to scratching. Speed may vary from 200 rpm to 1000 rpm for a 6″ lap. If troubled with persistent scratching, it is well to experiment with changes of speed. Generally around 400 rpm is satisfactory.

6. Pressure is a big factor in scratching. Pressure is due to vary with the size of the facet, the larger ones permitting more pressure than the small ones. But there often seems to be a fairly definite pressure which for a given facet gives best results, and variations in pressure either upward or downward will react unfavorably.

7. Untrue or wobbly laps may cause scratching.

8. When polishing a large facet such as a table on a large brilliant set on the faceting tool, and scratches persist, the stone may often be, to good advantage, taken off the faceting tool and held against the lap by hand. A little practice is needed to do

this effectively. The resulting facet may not be positively flat but will not be rounded enough to be noticeable.

9. When scratching persists on a large facet, it may sometimes be eliminated by turning the gem either 90° or 180° and polishing in the new direction. This is especially noted in gems having weak structure in their cleavage planes.

The cutting procedure outlined as standard is not a fast process. If one is going to cut large gems, it will pay to have a second cast iron lap to be used with No. FF carbo or even No. 150 carbo for doing the first coarse cutting of the main facets only. Or one may use the reverse side of his regular cutting lap if he is careful to wash all loose abrasive off it before using again with the No. 600 carbo.

In cutting and in polishing facets it is necessary to have a fairly correct idea of the time that elapses after a facet has been placed against the lap so that it may not be overcut nor overheated and so that time will not be lost through continuing the polishing after the condition of the facet is satisfactory. This is quite important. In polishing small facets they are often completed in from 5 to 6 seconds. If the worker allows his mind to wander for 15 seconds while working on such a small facet he may seriously overcut it. The Author takes care of this by making a habit of counting (not aloud) the seconds from the beginning of an operation. A little practice will enable one to count seconds quite accurately, though it does not make any difference if the count is in seconds just so that it is fairly regular. On the first of a series of facets of a given size one determines that the polishing requires, say, a count of 5. Then on succeeding facets the count of five means "time to inspect."

Abrasives for Polishing.—Most of these are mentioned in connection with the polishing of the particular gem on which their use seems to be indicated. However, a summarization of them in one place may be convenient for reference.

Tin Oxide is the most popular and most generally used abrasive for polishing. It is suitable for nearly all gems of all hardnesses from 5 up to but not including 9.

Tripoli is probably, next to tin oxide, the most widely used polishing medium. It is especially suitable for the stones around 8 in hardness.

Chromium oxide (green rouge) is used interchangeably with tin oxide.

Titanium oxide is used interchangeably with tin oxide.

"Putty Powder" is sometimes used in place of tin oxide. It seems that putty powder has no definite and fixed content but that its composition is dependent on the whim of the maker. It has a base of tin oxide or zinc oxide and contains an acid, probably always oxalic acid. It is excellent material for marble workers, but is inferior to tin oxide for gem polishing.

Damascus Ruby Powder is a patented preparation especially suited to certain of the gem materials which yield undue scratching when treated with tin oxide. Among these are, topaz, zircon, olivine. The formula is secret but analysis indicates that it is finely divided corundum, actually "ruby powder." One should not be frightened by the high price of this material, as an ounce of it will last the ordinary amateur a year or more.

Rottenstone is sometimes used for polishing corundum.

Carborundum Buffing Powder A No. 1 Fine, is used in place of both tin oxide and ruby powder. While it seems to work satisfactorily on nearly all gems, especially the harder ones, the Author has not found it especially preferable to either the tin oxide or the ruby powder except that on certain harder stones such as garnet it is much faster than the tin oxide. It has only recently been recognized as a suitable abrasive for this purpose, and the Author's experience with it is too limited to form a good basis of opinion.

Alumina (made by the Norton Co.) is apparently about the same thing as the Carbo Buffing Powder already referred to. The same notes apply.

CHAPTER VII

THE OPTICS OF BRILLIANTS

The man who expects to cut worth-while gems must learn something of the physical properties of gem material and the behavior of light in them. When these things are known, he can intelligently study the design of gems for the purpose of determining the best shape and proportions to give to those of each particular material.

The subject is one that is much neglected even by many professional lapidaries. Most writers who have occasion to mention the subject pass over it lightly. This attitude is wrong. Some writers have made statements about it that are decidedly misleading. We may determine satisfactory shapes and proportions with a fair degree of accuracy by the measurement of existing cut gems and from rather sketchy information published on the subject. But the man who tries to go to the bottom of each problem and understand causes and effects is the man who is most likely to produce outstanding work and is most likely to enjoy his work to the fullest extent. We all know that the cutter by skillful design can bring out the best that is in a stone and that by carelessness or ignorance he can ruin a good piece of material. We have all seen gems of most mediocre material that were beautiful. And we have seen gems of finest material that were "dead" or "sleepy" or only spotted with light. The cutter of the pleasing gem had utilized his knowledge of how light would behave when it entered the gem. The cutter of the poorer gem had either neglected or ignored the known laws, and the light entering the gem had not been controlled effectively. Within reasonable limits the cutter has control over the entering light. He can bring most of it out through the crown, which condition is desirable. He can further determine if most of it is to emerge through the side facets or through the table. Actually, for effectiveness the emerging light should be well distributed between the side facets and the table so that some facet or group of facets will appear brilliant when viewed from any one of many positions.

A complete and exact analysis of the paths of light through a gem is impossible. For a given condition of light source and point of observation such analysis can be made. But in practice the light enters the gem from an infinite number of directions and the emerging rays will be viewed from an infinite number of positions. To repeat this in other words (for it is important that this be remembered) if light entered the gem always from one or several fixed positions, and the gem was always viewed from one or several predetermined places, the shape and proportion necessary to produce the best effect could be readily determined once and for all, and henceforth all gems of the particular refractive index could be cut to that one pattern.

The conditions mentioned make it impossible to design an ideal gem. And so long as this is the case, there will be differences of opinion as to what cutting is most effective. In addition to the mentioned conditions there are many factors that enter into the design of a gem. Among these are the refractive index and the critical angle of the material, the inclination of both front and rear facets, the ratio of depth of crown to depth of pavillion, the width of the table, the sizes of the facets, the depth of color in the gem, etc. Before our study has progressed very far it will be readily apparent that any design arrived at and approved for any particular material must be very much a compromise between conflicting factors.

It is only by a careful study of many shapes and proportions and the graphic portrayal of the behavior of light in each that one can get a real picture of what happens to light in a transparent gem. This chapter is not intended as an authoritative treatise on the optics of gems. Its purpose is to call attention to the importance of the study and to try to direct the method of procedure necessary to the analysis of light behavior in a gem, so that anyone may undertake the work even though he may have had no previous training in physics.

Certain gems are cut for color only, no brilliancy being wanted. Among these is the emerald. We will not discuss these gems as, with them, the proportion is determined largely by whether the color is to be made as light as possible, in which case the gem is cut thin, or if it is to be as intense as possible, in which case the gem will be cut with considerable depth so as to increase the length of the path of the light rays through it. The white gem is invariably cut for brilliancy. The lightly tinted gem usually the same way. It is with this class that we will deal.

In undertaking our study we should realize that the gem materials with which we are dealing have certain fixed physical characteristics and the light with which we are dealing always obeys certain laws. Any text book on physics has a chapter on optics. This should be studied and must be studied if one's understanding of the matter is to be at all complete. But such texts are not always readily understandable to the man who has not studied physics.   It is not always easy for him to select and learn the essentials and to pass over the non-essentials. This discussion is to be kept as simple a possible, and many of the laws of light will not be mentioned at all, because they will not be worth, in this study, the confusion that they might introduce. Our procedure is to be first, a discussion of the principles that must be known before any gem fashioning is attempted, then an application of these principles to the design of effective gems. The essential laws, facts and definitions are few and simple, but they must be thoroughly understood.

The Crown of a gem is that portion of the gem above the girdle.

The Girdle of a gem is the edge that bounds the widest part of the gem.

The Pavillion of a gem is that portion of the gem below the girdle.

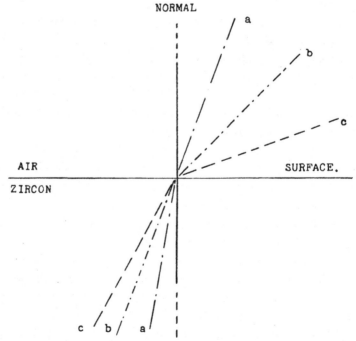

Figure 33.—SHOWING ACTUAL AMOUNT OF BENDING OF A LIGHT RAY PASSING FROM AIR TO ZIRCON.

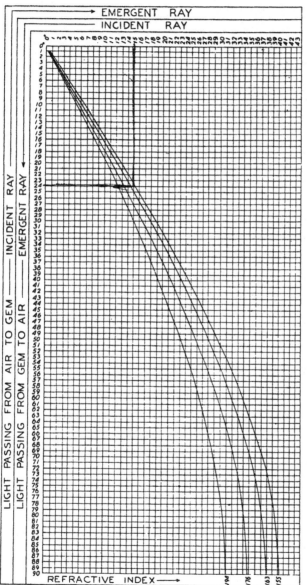

Figure 34.—CHART OF BEHAVIOR OF LIGHT IN THE PRINCIPAL GEM MATERIALS.

The Refractive Index of a material is the indication of the amount that a ray of light will bend when passing from air into the material.   Air is taken as a standard with a refractive index of 1.00.   When a ray of light passes from air into quartz with a refractive index of 1.55, it will be bent a certain amount. (The determination of this amount will be taken up later).   If a ray passes from air into topaz with a refractive index of 1.62, it will change its direction more than when it entered the quartz. It is to be noted and remembered that there is one condition under which there is no bending of the ray.   That is when the ray passing from one material into another strikes the inter-secting surface ·at an angle of 90° to that surface, there is no bending but the ray continues in a straight line.   Also bear in mind that the amount of bending at the surface is not a fixed value for each material but that it varies with the angle of incidence, ranging from 0° bending when the ray enters at 90° from the surface to as much as 50° of bend in the case of light entering quartz parallel to the surface, and still greater amounts of bending in materials of higher refractive indices.   Fig. 33 illustrates this.   The Chart Fig. 34 shows the exact amount of

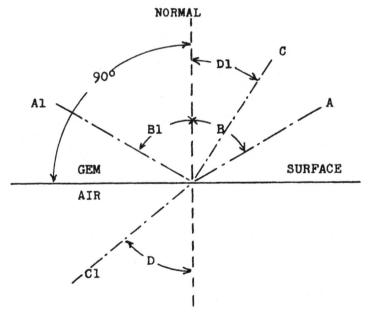

Figure 35.—ILLUSTRATING REFLECTION AND REFRACTION.

bending for each value of incident ray for the principal gem materials.

Reflection is what takes place if a ray of light strikes a surface and "glances off" instead of entering the material which it struck.

Refraction is what takes place if a ray of light strikes a surface and enters the material (along a new path) instead of being reflected. As mentioned before, unless the ray struck the surface at 90° from the surface, it will change its direction at the intersecting surface.

The Normal is a perpendicular erected at the point where a ray of light strikes a surface. See Fig. 35.

The Angle of Incidence is the angle with the normal made by a light ray where it strikes a surface. Angle B Fig. 35 is the Angle of Incidence of ray A.

The Angle of Reflection is the angle made with the normal by the reflected ray. Angle B-1 is the angle of reflection of ray A in Fig. 35. The angle of reflection is always equal to the angle of incidence. (Angle B-1=Angle B in Fig. 35).

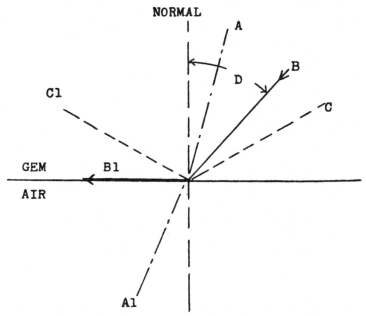

Figure 36.—ILLUSTRATING THE MEANING OF "CRITICAL ANGLE."

The Angle of Refraction is the angle with the normal made by a refracted ray of light. Light passing from air into a gem will always change its direction at the surface and will bend toward the normal. Light passing from a gem into air will change its direction at the surface and will bend away from the normal. Therefore, the angle of refraction is never equal to the angle of incidence but is always greater than or smaller than the angle of incidence. (In Fig. 35 angle D-1 is never equal to Angle D).

The Critical Angle is the angle with the normal, at which light traveling in a gem and striking a surface of the gem will neither be returned by reflection into the stone nor pass out into the air, but will, on striking a surface, coincide with it as B-1. Fig. 36. To repeat, Angle D is the critical angle of the material illustrated. Ray B, striking at just this angle, will change its direction to coincide with the surface of the gem. Ray A, striking at less than the critical angle, will pass out into the air as Ray A-1. Ray C, striking the surface at more than the critical angle, will be reflected back into the gem as ray C-1.

The rule for the determination of the critical angle is:

$$\frac{1}{\text{Refractive Index of Material}} = \text{Sine of Critical Angle}$$

Example: What is the critical angle of topaz? The refractive index of topaz is 1.62. 1, divided by 1.62 = .61728. From a table of sine functions we find that this figure is the sine of 38° 10' approx., which is the critical angle of topaz.

If a ray of light traveling in air strikes a gem, it will enter the gem. If it strikes at an angle other than normal, as we have already learned, it will bend toward the normal. The rule for the determination of the amount of its bending is:

$$\frac{\text{Sine of Angle of Incidence}}{\text{Refractive Index of Material}} = \text{Sine of Angle of Refraction}$$

Or, referring to Fig. 35:

$$\frac{\text{Sine Angle D}}{\text{Refractive Index of Material}} = \text{Sine Angle D-1}$$

Example: If light traveling through air strikes the surface of a topaz at 35° from the normal, at what angle with the normal will it enter the topaz? Substituting in the above formula, .57358 (the sine of 35°), divided by 1.62 (The refractive index of topaz) gives .35406, which is the sine of 20° 45' approximately, which is the angle with the normal at which the ray will enter the gem.

If a ray of light traveling in a gem strikes a surface at an angle with the normal smaller than the critical angle of the material, it will not be reflected but will be refracted out into the air. The ray will, as we have already learned, bend away from the normal. The rule for determining the amount of this bending is:

(Sine of Angle of Incidence) x (Refractive Index of Material) = (Sine of Angle of Refraction)

As an example of this, reverse the conditions of the last problem. If a ray of light traveling in topaz strikes a surface of air at an angle of 20° 45' from the normal, at what angle with the normal will it enter the air? Substituting in the formula just given, (.35406=the sine of 20° 45' x (1.62=refractive index of topaz) = (.57358 = the sine of 35°).

If a ray of light traveling in a gem strikes a surface of air at an angle greater than the critical angle of the material, it will be reflected back into the gem, and the angle of reflection will be equal to the angle of incidence.

The above definitions and formulae are the only ones necessary for the work contemplated. It is urged that the beginner in this study work out a few typical problems to get the rules well fixed in his mind. He should check his results against the chart Fig. 34. But for convenience in actual work the chart Fig. 34 is given. It plots with fair accuracy, and for refractive indices most commonly met with in gems, the amount of bending of light when it passes from air into gem and from gem into air. The critical angle of each material may be read directly above the intersection of the refractive index curve with the 90° line. For example, what is the refractive index of quartz? Reading upward from the intersection of the 1.55 line with the 90° line we find the answer "slightly above 40°."

To show the application of the rules involved it is worth while for us to work out one diagram of a brilliant gem. Suppose it is desired to know what proportions should be used for a round brilliant of quartz. Quartz has a refractive index of 1.55 and a critical angle just above 40°. Begin by drawing a section through an assumed and arbitrarily taken shape. We will incline the rear facets 41° from the girdle, because (as we will find later) if we make this angle any more acute, light entering the table at normal will pass on through the rear facets, and this we do not want. We will incline the front facets 45° from the girdle. See Fig. 37. Use a protractor for laying out all angles of gem and of light paths. Let the crown be 1/2 as deep as the pavil-

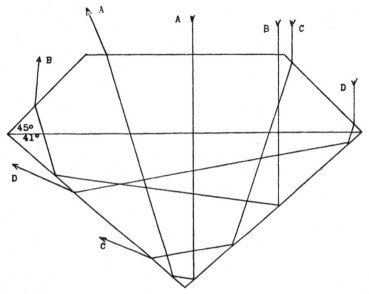

Ray	Strikes Gem	Enters Gem	Strikes First Surface	Strikes Second Surface	Strikes Third Surface	Leaves Gem
A	Normal	Normal	41°	56°	15°	24°
B	Normal	Normal	41°	56°	30°	51°
C	45°	27°	59°	38°		72°
D	45°	27°	59°	38°		72°

Figure 37.—PATHS OF PRINCIPAL RAYS THROUGH QUARTZ
WITH LIGHT ENTERING AT NORMAL.

lion. To avoid confusion show the rays entering only one half
of the crown area.   Draw ray A, striking at normal and entering
at normal.   (Keep in mind that all figures given in tracing these
rays are angles with the normal). Ray A strikes the first interior
surface at 41° and is reflected at 41°.   It strikes the second
surface at 56° and is reflected at 56°.   It then strikes the interior
surface at 15° and as this is less than the critical angle of quartz
the ray is going to pass out into the air.   Reference to the chart
shows that when light traveling in a gem with refractive index of
1.55 strikes a surface at an angle of 15° with the normal it will
pass into the air at an angle of 24° with the normal.

Ray B is traced in the same way and presents no new conditions.   Ray C is different in that it strikes the gem at an angle

of 45°. Again referring to the chart we find that this ray will enter the gem at an angle of 27° with the normal. From this step there is nothing new in the tracing of ray C. Ray D is similar. When the paths are all traced, it will be found that the light entering the main side facets is all lost out the back of the gem, and that all light entering the table comes out of the crown fairly well distributed. We do note that none of the rays come back out the center of the table, and the stone may therefore have an "empty" look when light enters at the normal. (The light from the side facets can be practically all brought back through the crown when it enters at normal to the table, but this can be accomplished only by inclining the front side facets 35°

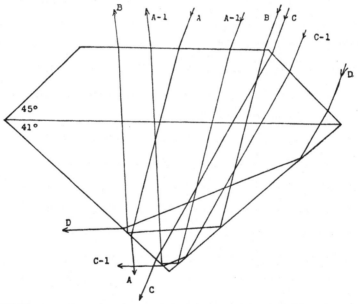

Ray	Strikes Gem	Enters Gem	Strikes First Surface	Strikes Second Surface	Strikes Third Surface	Leaves Gem
A	20°	13°				47°
A-1	20°	13°	54°	45°	5°	8°
B	20°	13°	54°	45°	5°	8°
C	25°	16°	12°			19°
C-1	25°	16°	70°	28°		47°
D	25°	16°	70°	28°		47°

Figure 38.—PATHS OF PRINCIPLE RAYS THROUGH QUARTZ WITH LIGHT ENTERING AT 20° FROM NORMAL.

from the girdle. This means either that the crown must be very shallow to maintain a table of reasonable size, or that the table be too small if the crown is of correct height. Either of these conditions constitutes a sacrifice not worth making, as the rays from the side facets will still be lost out the back as soon as the entering rays have moved only slightly from normal to the table.)

While the results are not ideal, we must keep in mind that the above is the picture of only one condition. Draw another diagram similar to the previous one and on it show the same series of rays all entering at 20° from normal to the table and see how the gem looks under this condition. It will be seen that the band of light leaving the crown has moved toward the center of the stone. Other diagrams should be drawn, using other shapes, and it is well to make three diagrams of each shape, filling in one with rays entering at 10° from normal to the table. Study of all shapes will probably convince the student that the shape assumed herein is about as effective as he can find for quartz.

As we pass to materials with higher refractive indices it becomes increasingly easy to make more and more of the entering rays effective.

In actual practice drawings should be made with the girdle at least eight inches wide to insure reasonable accuracy of the angles. Drawings should be made of whatever gem is to be investigated. By repeated trials with varied inclinations of both front and rear facets and keeping in mind the ideal conditions of distribution already set forth, the best design may be chosen.

The Author does not propose to express decided opinions as to the best shapes and proportions for the round brilliants we have been discussing. Each cutter has his own ideas. This is as it should be, and it is for the purpose of stimulating investigation and the formulation of ideas that this chapter was written. It is suggested that investigation be conducted in the following way: divide all the commonly used gem materials into four groups and use as the refractive index of each group a figure that is an average of the refractive indices of all the gems within that group. Then use this average figure as the refractive index of any gem within that group. This cannot of course give strictly correct results, but is in most cases nearly enough correct to use in general investigations. The Chart of Light Behavior, Fig. 34, only gives the four refractive indices referred to. These are, 1.55 for quartz, beryl, etc.; 1.63 for topaz, tourmaline, etc.; 1.76 for garnets, corundum, etc.; and 1.94 for zircon. If it is desired to draw a strictly correct diagram for one of the materials with a refractive index considerably removed from the average figures given here, the functions can be gotten from the chart with sufficient accuracy by interpolation.

As a starting point for investigations and as fair and usable designs for each of the four groups, the following proportions are suggested:

For gems of R. I.   1.55 incline rear main facets 41° from the girdle; front main facets 45°.   The height of the crown to be 1/2 the height of the pavillion.

For gems of R. I.   1.63 incline rear main facets 39°; front main facets 43°.   Height of crown to be 1/2 the height of pavillion.

For gems of R. I.   1.76 incline rear main facets 42°; from main facets 37°.   Height of crown to be 1/3 the height of pavillion.

For gems of R. I.   1.94 incline rear main facets 40°; front main facets 43°.   Height of crown to be 1/2 height of pavillion.

CHAPTER VIII

ORIENTATION OF GEM TO CRYSTAL

Most gems do not require any attention to orientation. With some of them this is most important. Some require this care on account of their cleavage, some because of dichroism, and some because their color is not evenly distributed in the crystal.

Topaz.—This material has a distinct cleavage at right angles to the long axis of the crystal. It is very important that the gem cut from topaz be so oriented that this cleavage will not be parallel to any facet, especially a large facet and more especially the table. Also, it is well not to turn the axis of the gem $90°$ from the axis of the crystal, as this puts the cleavage parallel to the axis of the gem, increasing the tendency for flakes to cleave off the thin girdle. The best orientation for topaz is probably with the axis of the gem inclined about $15°$ from the axis of the crystal.

Kunzite and Hiddenite.—Has very distinct cleavage parallel to the long axis. Professional cutters work it with the table at right angles to the long axis of the crystal. It is presumed that they have found by experience that this is better than inclining the axis of the gem somewhat from the axis of the crystal, as might seem to be the better scheme.

Tourmaline.—This material is always cut with the table of the gem parallel to the long axis of the crystal. If a gem is cut with its table at right angles to the long axis of the crystal, the gem will almost invariably be either opaque or too dense in color, or will have a color (usually unpleasing) quite different from the one seen in looking through the side of the crystal. Usually this color will be a dingy yellow or brown.

Sapphire.—The color in sapphire is seldom distributed evenly. Almost always it is in spots and often in rather small spots with the rest of the stone a white or cream color. When this condition exists, it is highly important that the gem be so oriented that the best color spot be located in the culet of the gem and placed as symmetrically as possible. The Eastern native cutter is notorious for invariably cutting for weight only and with total disregard for optical considerations. His gems are re-cut in America or Europe to make them more symmetrical and to give them better optical properties. The American or European cutter must examine such gems carefully, as it sometimes happens that cutting them to proper symmetry removes the color spot and ruins the gem.

Amethyst.—Amethyst is like sapphire in the matter of color distribution, and the same precautions must be used. In buying rough amethyst crystals or lumps careful examination pays. The rock crystal usually grows out from a parent mass that is opaque. At the junction of the opaque mass and the clear quartz is usually a band of semi-clear material filled with opaque spots and having many fractures. Even though the entire crystal presents to the casual observer a uniform pleasing amethyst color, the color is often actually a spot back in the semi-clear section, while all the unflawed material is clear white. It sometimes happens (though not often) that attractive cabochons can be cut from such specimens.

Chapter IX

MOSAICS

The making of mosaics is interesting work, and if done well, the product is attractive. It is better to start with simple geometric designs and work into picture mosaics later. Many schemes and short cuts will suggest themselves to the worker as he studies designs and the best way of executing them. This chapter is merely to call attention to the work as an interesting one and to point out the treatments on which a sound technique may be built. Basically the whole work consists of :

Cutting the material to shape.
Cementing the pieces together.
Cutting the desired shape from the cemented mass.

Stones for ring sets, brooches, etc. are good subjects for beginners. Assume that it is desired to make a ring set of the simplest possible form of mosaic, namely, alternate strips of materials of contrasting colors. Let us choose red and green agate. The material should if possible be similar or closely related in hardness and polishing characteristics. If one is very hard and the other soft, the soft material may undercut to a noticeable extent. Let us make the first stone about 3/4" long by 1/2" wide with a red center strip and green areas at both ends. Cut one cube of red agate 1/4" x 1/4" x 1/2". Cut two of the same size of green agate. Cut a piece of ordinary window glass just more than 1/2" x 3/4" for a temporary base. The cubes are to be carefully squared on an iron lap with carbo paste, preferably about No. 150. The purpose of the coarse cut is to provide a rough surface for the cement. One side of the glass is to be rough ground for the same reason.

Cementing these together can be done in any of many ways but the Author has not found any other as satisfactory as the Bakelite Resin scheme. A one pound can of BR 0014 Resinoid can be gotten from The Bakelite Corporation, 247 Park Ave., New York City. The pieces of agate and the roughened side of the piece of glass are all coated heavily with the resin, the blocks are assembled in proper order on the piece of glass and the whole assembly put in an oven to bake. It is to be baked for 24 hours at a temperature of about 100° C. The temperature should then be lowered to about 50 or 60° for an hour or two. The current is then cut off and the stone left in the oven to cool as the oven cools. The oven may be made at home at little expense.

One that has done good service is made of a sheet metal, one pound candy box about 5″ x 8″ x 3″ with hinged cover. A hole is drilled in one end to admit a lamp cord to which an ordinary lamp socket is connected in the box. A 60 watt lamp is the heating element. A second hole is drilled in the end of the box for the insertion of a Centigrade thermometer with a 110° scale. The temperature is controlled by raising or lowering the lid. The oven referred to gives the correct temperature with the lid open about 1/2″ at its highest point. Obviously the arrangement would not be satisfactory if close regulation were required, but it is adequate for this job. Also obviously a standard laboratory oven is a better device for this job, but many of us do not have these ovens and will not want them often enough to justify their purchase.

After the stone has cooled, it is cemented on a lap stick and cut just as if it were a cabochon of solid material. After the front has been cut and polished, it is removed from the lap stick and the glass base is ground off on an iron lap and the base of the gem finished in the regular way.

If the assembly forming the pattern is as much as 3/16″ thick, it can be worked without being attached to a base, but if the stone is very thin, there is danger of the joints giving way unless it is reinforced by a base.

In grinding and polishing use only true wheels without bumps on them, and do not crowd the work. Take your time.

In squaring the cubes be careful that no chipped places are left at the edges.

The pattern may be made of thin slabs laid flat on a permanent base. If this is done, the base should be of agate or some tough stone, so that it may have the necessary strength without excessive thickness.

When the polishing is finished, the joints, if not perfect, will be slightly undercut, due to the softness of the bakelite. Polishing powder may get into such joints. It may be removed by short periods of polishing on a dry clean lap made of a piece of wool carpet installed against the side of a wool wheel, or on the periphery of a clean cloth lap.

CHAPTER X

IMPREGNATION OF GEM MATERIALS

The mineralogist often finds materials which he would like to examine microscopically in section but which are so soft and crumbly that he cannot cut a clear section. He corrects this condition by impregnating the specimen with bakelite, then cutting and polishing the impregnated surface.

While the Author has not experimented extensively with this scheme as applied to gems, he has used it enough to determine definitely that it has value in many cases. Due to lack of data a detailed and specific technique cannot be given, but it is proposed to give such information as is available in the belief that it will furnish a groundwork on which the amateur lapidary can build a satisfactory treatment.

M. N. Short in his "Microscopic Determination of the Ore Minerals," published as U. S. Geological Survey Bulletin 825, gives the following:

"The specimen is immersed in a dish containing the solution of bakelite in ether and alcohol or ether and acetone. The bakelite should be thinned to about the consistency of a thin watery syrup. The dish is covered to prevent too rapid evaporation of the solvent. The bakelite solution is drawn into the pores of the specimen by capillarity. After four to eight hours the cover is taken off the dish, and the contents are exposed to the air overnight. The solution is then about the consistency of unthinned bakelite or possibly still thicker. The specimen is then removed from the dish and placed with its flat side uppermost in a warming oven. Care should be taken to have a generous coating of the solution on the surface and to keep the surface horizontal so that the solution will not run off. A temperature of approximately 40°C. is maintained for about 24 hours. The temperature is then gradually raised to about 110°C. and maintained there an additional 24 hours. At the end of that time the bakelite is hard and resembles amber. It is futile to attempt to hasten the process of curing bakelite. The application of too much heat or a too rapid increase in the heat will cause its decomposition and the formation of bubbles, which will tend to blow out material already in the pores. The excess bakelite is ground off the surface on a horizontal lap with F Carborundum. The specimen is then examined under the microscope. If impregnation has not been sufficient, the entire process can be repeated, as cured bakelite is not affected by the solvent used

* * * * * The method above described is, in the writer's opinion, the best method yet devised for impregnating a specimen."

A request to the Bakelite Corporation, 247 Park Ave., New York, N. Y., brought the following brief description of the preparation of rock sections for miscroscopic study:

"A thin section of the rock is embedded in plaster of paris or magnesite cement to give it support during the impregnation. When the cast has set, it is coated with Bakelite BR 0014 and baked for 2 hours at 85°C. The temperature is then increased to 95° to 100°C. and maintained for 8 to 10 hours. It is then allowed to cool slowly, after which a slide may be cut in the same manner as from a piece of tough igneous rock. The grains will not pull out of the matrix nor will the slide chip around the edges."

There are certain discrepancies in the two accounts. The Author does not propose to try to reconcile them, as they are of such nature that they need not interfere with free experimentation on the part of the individual worker, and through such experimenting each worker will arrive at his own conclusions,

There are certain gem materials, such as turquoise, with soft matrix that are vastly improved by treatment with an impregnating medium. The Author's brief tests have been made as follows, using turquoise in matrix as a subject:

Grind the gem to shape in the regular way. Let the final grinding operation be one employing loose grains of abrasive such as Carborundum grains on a wood wheel. The loose abrasive tends to undercut the matrix, which is desirable as it gives a better body to the bakelite that will replace the crumbled matrix. Coat the gem with Bakelite Resinoid BR 0014. Bake for 12 hours at about 100°C. Cool slowly. Polish with fine pumice on soft felt and finish with tin oxide on soft felt.

Many amateurs do not have ovens. An oven that is not at all accurate as to control but that will be satisfactory for such jobs as this one, can be readily made at home. Take a sheet metal box 3" x 5" x 8" or thereabouts, with a hinged cover. Drill two holes in an end. Into one of these holes insert a lamp cord and connect it to it an ordinary brass lamp socket. Use a 60 watt lamp as a heating element. Into the other hole is inserted a centigrade thermometer with a 110° scale. Temperature control is gotten with sufficient accuracy by raising or lowering the hinged cover. Actual test must determine the size of the crack to be left at the lid for any given temperature, but as an indication, the Author's "oven" shows the desired temperature with a 1/4" crack of the lid.

When the surface of the specimen is curved, which is nearly always the case, the bakelite tends to run off the specimen until the deposit is not heavy enough to insure a smooth cut surface. If this trouble is foreseen, the specimen may be placed in a narrow vessel (made of wood or of tin), just larger than the gem, and the bakelite poured over it until the gem is submerged. Then when the baking is complete, the gem is encased in a block of bakelite. The bakelite is ground away on a carbo wheel until the ground surface approaches the gem surface. Then the finishing is done as outlined above.

The bakelite has an amber color; so all deposits of it left in or on the gem will be amber colored.

CHAPTER XI

THE ARTIFICIAL COLORING OF AGATES*

By E. V. Van Amringe

Chemical treatment of agates and other forms of chalcedony to enhance their natural color began at Idar, Germany, about 1820. It is quite impossible that the art was known to the ancients, although it may have been practiced by the Italian cameo workers of the Middle Ages. Certainly no specimen of artificially colored material of great age has survived to us. At present, however, the great majority of commercial agates possess a far more brilliant color than that imparted to them by nature. Banded forms of chalcedony are most successfully treated, as the layers differ considerably in porosity, and therefore in the quantity of coloring matter they will absorb.

Black was the first color produced. The well dried stone is soaked for two to three weeks in dilute sugar solution (13 ozs. sugar to 1 quart of water) or honey solution or olive oil. The temperature should be moderately warm. The stone is then washed, immersed in concentrated sulphuric acid, and slowly warmed for one hour. Then the acid is carefully boiled from fifteen minutes to one hour. This rather dangerous operation may be avoided by allowing the stone to remain in the warm acid for one hour and cooling and repeating the warming process. If too intense color is obtained, it may be softened by treatment with nitric acid. To keep the stone from "sweating," it should be carefully washed and dried for several days at a moderate temperature. The black color is of course due to carbonization of the organic compound, and the effect produced resembles closely the true onyx.

Red is generally formed by ignition after immersion in iron nitrate solution. This is prepared by dissolving eight ounces of iron nails in two pounds of concentrated nitric acid, the product being decanted until clear. The stones are soaked in this liquid for two weeks, for those about 2 mm. thick, to four weeks for those about 10 mm. thick. Success is seldom obtained with thicker specimens, and drying and repetition of the process is recommended in all cases. After the agate is thoroughly soaked with the iron salt, it is dried at gentle heat for from two

---

*This paper is reprinted from the Bulletin of the Mineralogical Society of Southern California with the permission of the Publisher and the Author. We are grateful to them for their kind permission.

to ten days, according to thickness, and without cooling heated red hot in a closed crucible. Both the ignition and the final cooling must be slowly and evenly performed if fracture of the stone is to be avoided. Artificial carnelian and sardonyx are the result.

Blue color is produced by soaking the stone in a luke warm solution of potassium ferrocyanide (yellow prussiate of potash) (9 ozs. to 1 qt. of water) for one or two weeks. After washing, the agate is left for eight or ten days in a saturated solution of ferrous sulfate, rewashed and dried slowly. The latter process may be repeated until the desired shade is obtained. A darker color results from the addition of both concentrated sulfuric and nitric acids to the ferrous sulfate solution, or potassium ferricyanide (red prussiate of potash) may be substituted for the yellow prussiate. These blue chalcedonys are the so-called German or Swiss lapis, or imitation lapis lazuli.

Green of a bluish shade results from immersion in a saturated solution of potassium dichromate for from one week to two months (for stones of one half inch in thickness). The specimen is then transferred to a closed container and exposed to the fumes from lump ammonium carbonate for two weeks. After drying, it is gradually and strongly heated until the desired tint is produced. Apple green color is obtained from a similar procedure in a solution of nickle nitrate. The ammonium carbonate treatment may be omitted. The resulting stones resemble chrysoprase.

Brown of a rich hue, giving the appearance of some garnets, is produced by soaking the material in brown sugar for some time, and then carefully igniting.

Yellow of a lemon shade results from continued digestion in warm crude concentrated hydrochloric acid or potassium dichromate solution.

Fancy Colors obtained by simple dyeing with aniline dyes inevitably fade on exposure to light and eventually disappear.

A general procedure which must be followed in every experiment in artificial coloring is the careful removal from the specimen of oils or substances of an undesirable color. This may be accomplished by a bath in a caustic soda solution, followed by drying and soaking in warm dilute nitric acid for two or three days. The acid should finally be brought to boiling. Continued repetition of this procedure may be necessary to completely free the stone from iron and other stains.

CHAPTER XII

SOFT CARVING (WITH STEEL TOOLS)

The man with a reasonably developed sense of perspective can find much pleasure in carving either full figures or full relief or bas relief in soft minerals. This article will deal only with bas relief carving. It is not different from either of the other kinds of carving, and it will be less confusing to describe only the one kind. The writer does not propose to attempt to give detailed instructions. It is not necessary. The desire is to outline the general method to such extent that the beginner can with study and practice develop an individual satisfactory technique. The presentation of this chapter is made possible by the kindness of Mr. Albert H. Bumstead, who has done a considerable amount of such work and who was most liberal with instructions. Mr. Bumstead finds in this work a satisfaction that gem cutting was not quite able to give. This doubtless indicates that he is an artist as well as an artisan, and such a man will find in this work plenty of opportunities for the exercise of the artistic sense. The almost purely mechanical job of gem cutting does not offer such opportunities. Mr. Bumstead's specialty is the transferring of photographs to bas reliefs in marble. He does this with such correctness and with such fineness of detail that the fidelity of his reproductions is truly amazing. He uses a camera lucida to project the image of the photograph onto the marble. This scheme is, we believe, original with him and is a distinctly valuable contribution.

The carving of any figure requires on the part of the worker a very detailed knowledge of the shape of the figure. Those of us who think that we are observant are subject to a rude awakening when we first attempt to carve, let us say, a bas relief of a human face. It is remarkable how little we know of the detailed shape of the face. But, fortunately, faces are rather plentiful and we can always get a friend or some member of our own family to pose for us long enough to allow us to grasp the detail that is obscure.

Let us begin with a bas relief in marble. Let us make it a human face or face, neck and shoulders. It is better to choose a photograph in profile as this is much more simple to work than a full face. There will be required for the work:

A rigid table or work bench.

A slab of soft white marble about 6" x 4 1/2" x 3/4".

A camera lucida with adjustable holder.

An easel for holding the photograph.

2 "C" clamps for clamping marble slab to table, or the slab may be held in a neat fitting socket made of wood cleats tacked to the bench on 4 sides of the slab.

A light hammer.

A straight cold chisel, preferably about 1/4" x 8".

A depth guage consisting of a piece of straight dressed wood about 1/2" x 1/2" x 10" with a small nail through it at about its center.

Several engraving tools of different shapes and of proper temper for carving in the marble. These should be made at home or by a blacksmith, of about 3/16" tool steel or drill rod. The shapes should be: 1 heavy flat, 1 light flat, 1 cape, 1 round nosed, 1 diamond point. Each of these tools to be fitted with a graver handle such as Dixon's Fig. S-2184.

Several die sinkers riffle files. Dixon's Fig. S-1766, numbers 1, 3, 5, 7, 11, 14 are recommended.

Medium fine sandpaper for final smoothing.

A word as to making and tempering the tools. The forming and tempering of steel tools has been described many times, but for the sake of convenience we insert a brief description. The tools are first heated and forged to approximate shape. The heating may be done with a gasoline blow torch or over the flame of a gas stove. Steel in small pieces burns quite easily, and care must be taken not to overheat it. When the tools have cooled in the open air, they are ground or filed to exact shape. Then they are hardened. This is done by heating the point to a cherry red and plunging in cold water. Hold them in the water until they are cold. They are now glass hard and would break in use; so some of the hardness must be taken out. Rub a side of the tool with sandpaper· until it is bright at and back from the point. Hold the tool in such position in the flame that the heat is applied back away from the point of the tool. Observe the color of the bright portion carefully. When a band of light straw yellow moves along the bright portion and reaches the end of the tool, plunge in water or oil. Tools as small as these are hard to temper properly because the temperature changes so rapidly. It is hard to observe the color changes when the tool is held in a bright flame. With a little practice this necessity can be eliminated. Heat the tool until it is consideraly hotter than is correct for tempering. Dip the end of the tool in water to cool it. Then as the point warms again from the heat stored in the main body of the tool, the light straw yellow band will be seen moving relatively slowly toward the end of the tool. When it reaches the end, the tool is to be plunged in water or oil.

The photograph from which the carving is to be made may be that of a friend or it may be taken from the roto-gravure section of a newspaper or from one of many magazines such as "movie" magazines.

For the size of slab specified, the finished carving should be about 3" x 4". It is well to have the photograph about the same size, though the size of the image can be varied by changing the distance of the photograph from the camera lucida.

Put the slab in its socket on the bench or clamp it in place with C clamps. Set the camera lucida directly above the center of the slab and about 12" from the slab. Set the easel with its photograph in place, directly in front of the camera lucida and about 12" away from it. This spacing gives an image the size of the photograph. If the carving is to be larger than the photograph, the easel is moved nearer to the camera lucida. If the carving is to be smaller than the photograph, the easel is moved further away. Some final adjusting will have to be done to make the image of just the right size and to get it placed right on the marble slab. After this has been done, several reference points should be drawn on the photograph at points somewhat remote from the figure to be carved, so that the corresponding points on the marble will not be cut away by the carving. These reference points may be small cross marks. Being certain that the image is in the proper place on the marble slab and that it is of the desired size, the reference points should be marked with scratches on the marble and made plain by marking the scratches with a black pencil. A good light should be so placed that it will brightly illuminate the photograph and leave the marble in shadows.

There is quite a "trick" to using the camera lucida for projecting a clear image and still permitting the worker to see the point of the cutting tool. The trick is to produce an image of just such intensity that details of it can be seen and that the carving tool is clearly visible at the same time. The trick must be learned by practice. Excellent practice is the copying of line sketches with a pen or pencil.

The first step is to outline the figure. Trace the outer boundary of the figure on the marble with a pencil. Then proceed to cut a channel about 3/4" wide all around the figure that is to be left in relief. The channel should be of uniform depth, and this depth should be about 1/4". See Fig. 39-A. The depth is to be checked with the wooden depth gauge. This channeling is done with the cold chisel and the light hammer.

A.

B.

Figure 39.—PLAN AND SECTION OF OUTLINE CHANNEL.

The cutting should be directed away from the outline marks. Then from a point about 3/4" away from the outline marks, the other side of the groove should be chiseled down to form a valley with sloping sides all around the figure. This valley will look like Fig. 39-B. Next, with the round nosed tool or with the diamond pointed tool, cut the base of the sloping side back toward the figure at point "A." Relieve the overburden occasionally with the flat tool until the bottom of the trench forms a true outline of the figure. The bottom of the trench should now be smoothed, using the flat tool.

At this point it is well to study the photograph at considerable length and plan very definitely the relationship of the various elevations. Remember that you are going to indicate a range in elevations of possibly 6" to 10" (depending on the position of the body relative to the head) and that it must be done with an actual difference in elevation of only 1/4". And that the various changes in elevation should be held to proportions as true as possible. There are exceptions to this statement, but it is in general correct. Sometimes a change in elevation must be exaggerated in order to be visible. In other cases it must be minimized in order not to devote too much of the limited depth to some feature that is not significant.

With a head in profile and the bust turned 45° from the head the point nearest the observer will be a shoulder. It may well be that the change in elevation from the shoulder to the side of the head will be as much as or more than the measurement from the side of the head to the base plane. But one half the total depth should not be given to the shoulder for two reasons. There is no detail to be shown on the shoulder, and also it is separated from the head by the valley of the neck and therefore can be only slightly higher than the side of the head and still give good effect. And this should be the treatment given, thereby leaving nearly all the 1/4" depth in which to work out the fine details of the head and face. The next highest portion of the figure will be either the hair or the ear. Next will come the side of the face, then the eye, then the low region adjacent to nose and mouth, and finally the nose and mouth.

The details of determining the various planes and the outlining of them and the actual carving of the figure are things that each worker must do as seems best to him. The writer does as little work as possible under the camera lucida, preferring to use this prism to correctly outline features on the marble with a pencil and to do the actual carving by direct observation. The procedure is in this case, after the outlines are marked, to cut channels with a round nosed tool, these channels to separate the various planes of elevation. These separating channels having been cut, the lowering of the various sections to their correct height is done with whatever tools seem most suitable. Generally coarse work should be done with either the flat tool or the roundnosed one, using a steady pressure and a slight rocking motion. When the cutting approaches a final surface, the flat tool pushed straight without rocking and almost flat on the work is used to fairly well smooth the surface. As any feature approaches completion, it should be either worked under the camera lucida or be frequently checked by this means.

The final shaping on delicate features such as eyes, nose, etc., as well as a final semi-smoothing of all surfaces, is done with a suitable shape of riffle file.

When all shaping is completed, the surfaces are smoothed with fine sandpaper.

The background may be finished either before or after the figure has been completed, but it is well to leave it at least until all rough carving has been done on the figure so that depths of cutting may be measured from it. The background may be either all removed down to a flat surface at the plane of the base of the figure, or the "outline ditch" may have its outer limits shaped symmetrically and its outer walls trued and smoothed, leaving all surrounding material at its original elevation. Or the removal may be done so as to leave a bead around the outer edge of the slab, thereby forming a frame for the carving.

A great deal depends on the marble chosen. A soft white compact marble without veins or readily visible crystals is best, in fact is necessary if good work is to be done. The marble must not be brittle, as this prevents the forming of sharp clean edges.

Except for the channeling around the whole figure, and the removing of surplus material beyond the outline of the figure, all cutting is done by pushing the tool by hand. A heavy pressure on the tool combined with a slight rocking motion will result in rapid removal of the material in the form of chips. A steady straight pressure will result in dust or fine grains, depending on the amount and direction of pressure.

CHAPTER XIII

CARVING AND ENGRAVING

In a previous chapter we discussed the carving of soft materials such as marble, alabaster, etc., using steel cutting tools propelled by hand. While the chapter dealt specifically with bas reliefs, it is of course understood that the same materials dealt with in the same way are suitable for all sorts of figurines, etc.

Carving and engraving of harder gem materials requires an entirely different equipment and method. Such cutting is done with revolving tools charged with diamond dust. As an approach to this work, which is so radically different from anything we have done before, it is suggested that considerable practice be gotten with similar shapes of tools made of Carborundum, using as a subject material something like malachite, just a little too hard to carve by hand yet perfectly workable with the Carborundum tools.

The lathe required for this soft carving with carbo points is identical with the one that will be needed for the hard carving except for the spindle. It is best to have this lathe made by a good machinist. Fig. 40 shows the essentials of this lathe. They are: a rigid base, rugged pedestals, adequate bearings of the adjustable pillow block type or ball bearings. The spindle may be 1/2" or larger. The driven pulley should be between the pedestals to prevent whipping of the shaft with slight wear

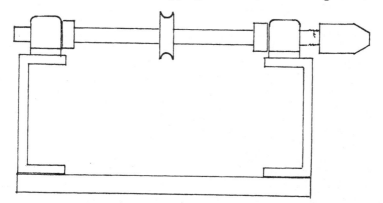

Figure 40.—ESSENTIALS OF LATHE FOR CARVING WITH CARBORUNDUM TOOLS.

of bearings. The spindle is to have adjustable collars to take up end play. The pedestals should be about 6" high to allow plenty of working space beneath the cutting tools. It is well to have a distance of about 10" between bearings. The spindle is to be turned true and threaded to take a good tripod chuck. Use a Jacobs or similar chuck. Do not waste money buying a cheap chuck, as it will not run true. An endless (glued) round belt is better than a belt with metal coupling, as the metal coupler gives a little jerk to the spindle.

The tools provided for cutting should include initially an assortment of mounted carbo discs and points such as Dixon's Fig. S2956 and 2957. There should also be an assortment of discs and wheels such as the Fig. S2957 unmounted. These wheels are used on mandrel shown in Fig. 2968. For very soft materials the various burs in Figs. S2959 to 2966 are useful.

The cutting is to be done with the above tools. The smoothing and polishing is done on home made tools. Make disc shaped tools of sizes convenient to mount on above mentioned mandrel. These are made of horn fibre, or hardwood or sole leather, and are used with No. FF carbo or No. 600 carbo or with pumice for the smoothing. Hard felt discs or leather discs with tin oxide are used for polishing. The shapes of both smoothing and polishing discs are to be varied so as to reach into any depressions that may have been cut. To accomplish this some tools will have to be made with sharp points and some with rounded points. These are made of wood rods and grasped directly in the chuck. The abrasives used on them are the same as the abrasives used on the discs for corresponding purpose. For very fine work in depressions small discs of felt or leather may be glued onto the ends of the rods and used with carbo or pumice or tin oxide.

The speed in all the above operations should be high. Ten thousand rpm would be more effective than lower speeds, but it takes a good lathe to stand this speed; so most of us will probably have to be content with speeds of around 5000 rpm.

We have deliberately refrained from trying to be specific in these instructions and the others to follow on the same subject. Each man must work out his own system. It is suggested that as the worker makes his experiments, he record them and state definitely if each was a success or a failure. No one can remember all his experiments, and this system of recording them will save much time by preventing duplication of old experiments.

The above work, if pursued a reasonable time, will teach the worker at a good speed and a low cost many things that he must know before he can produce good work in the harder stones with the diamond tools.

Assuming that the lathe has proven entirely satisfactory, it can now be adapted to the hard carving by the simple expedient of providing a new spindle. The head of this spindle is shown in Fig. 41 together with several points typical of those that will be required. These shapes are merely indicative. Actually a well equipped engraver's stand will have probably a hundred points. The points provided initially should be of approximately the shape and size that has been found most useful in the carbo points. The sketch is self explanatory. The points are made of steel turned to shape. When worn they may be reformed by heating and upsetting the ends, then turning the desired shape in the upset portion. Needless to say, the prime consideration

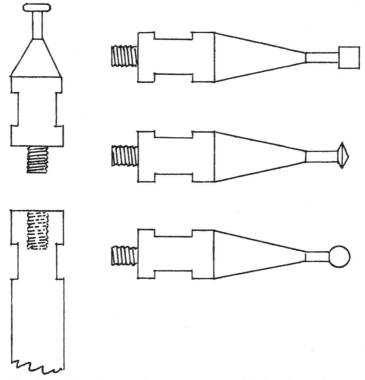

Figure 41.—SPINDLE HEAD WITH SEVERAL TYPICAL POINTS FOR CARVING WITH DIAMOND.

in this lathe and its point assembly is accuracy. The points must run true and without lost motion.

The points are charged with the diamond dust by touching them, while they are running, to a paste of diamond dust and oil. The professional engraver crushes the bortz in a mortar of steel with a steel pestle. The mortar and pestle consists essentially of a block of steel with a hole about 3/4" dia. drilled in it to a depth of about 3". The bottom of the hole is rounded (semi-spherical). A neat fitting steel rod with rounded end is the pestle and also the applicator. The bortz is crushed in this mortar with a small amount of olive oil, which with the dust forms a paste. The paste adheres to the pestle. It is applied to the cutting points by lifting the pestle from the mortar and touching it to the revolving point.

It is probably better for the amateur to buy such small amounts of diamond dust as he is likely to want. Spread one carat of it lightly with a film of oil, over an area about 1" x 2" or equivalent, on a hard steel surface such as the blade of a wood plane. Apply to the tool by touching this charged area to the cutting portion of the tool while the tool is revolving.

Here as in the previous job no attempt will be made to be specific. The worker should begin with fairly heavy tools and will therefore do only the coarser types of carving. As experience and skill are acquired in this coarser carving, the worker may go by degrees into the finer and more delicate work of gem engraving. The technique will be the same and the tools will be of the same form but much smaller and more delicate. Some of the disc shaped tools used in fine engraving are only a few hundredths of an inch in diameter and incredibly delicate. The fairly coarse engraving is done under an "engravers lens" mounted on a stand. For the finer work the engraver uses a loupe type of magnifier. The work naturally demands a good eye and a steady hand.

The polishing is done as was described in the paragraphs on carving with Carborundum. For some materials points of approximately the shape and size of the cutting points but made of tin are effective for polishing with tin oxide. Wood points will be used more freely on this work than on the softer carving where the felt and leather were more often effective.

The loss of diamond is not serious if one is not going to do a considerable amount of work. While frequent recharging is necessary, the amount of dust taken up by each charge is very small. However, the dust can be reclaimed. Set a large shallow pan under the cutting point and take care to wipe off all surplus dust into this pan. The pan of course also catches all dust that

is scraped off in actual grinding. The debris and dust in this
pan are occasionally washed out with benzine into a small glazed
earthenware vessel or a bowl of deep saucer shape, and the
batch is "panned" by washing just as gold is separated by
panning except that benzine is used instead of water.

CHAPTER XIV

DIAMOND POLISHING *

General Discussion

Not many amateur lapidaries will attempt the polishing of diamonds. The work is radically different from any described in connection with the softer stones. The equipment used for cutting other stones is not suitable here. The cost of raw material is more than many amateurs can afford to spend for experimental purposes. And certainly one should expect to spoil some good material before he can do any "pointing with pride." Yet the Author has seen some very attractive diamonds cut by amateurs. The job is not hopeless for the skilled amateur. The novice should let it alone. It is a job more tedious and more costly than appeals to most of us.

We cannot "teach" diamond polishing in one short chapter nor in a long volume. It is a job that each man must teach himself. Yet we can list a number of the things that must be done and the things that must not be done. We can list the material and equipment that is used. We can describe after a fashion the way in which the diamond worker uses it. We cannot tell just how the cleaver knows exactly where to scratch and cleave a crystal. We cannot give any formula for setting a dop so that exactly the right surface will be presented to the wheel. We cannot teach the beginner to mould the melted solder around the diamond with his bare fingers as the professional does it. But, we repeat, we can tell him what tools the diamond worker uses and how he uses them—the rest must be left to the initiative and judgment and ingenuity of the individual. These comments should not be taken as too discouraging. They are intended to be merely informative in that they point out that the diamond worker's road is not strewn with flowers. Each diamond worker must learn most features of the work for himself, no matter under how good a master he serves his apprenticeship. The master cannot tell him a great deal more than can be written in this description. True, the ability to see each job done by others is of enormous value. Yet the inability to see the operations performed by skilled workmen is not an insuperable barrier.

*For the detailed information contained in this Chapter we are indebted to Arthur A. Crafts Co. and to Mr. F. L. Huston especially. Without the help of Mr. Huston this Chapter could not have been presented.

We propose to discuss the work as fully as possible with complete realization of our inability to make all points clear, and with the full knowledge that after we have given all the information we can put on paper, the beginner must still work out for himself some of the most serious problems.

The diamond should be cut to a full brilliant form as was described in the chapter on faceting. The angle of inclination of its facets is different from any discussed in that chapter. Many formulas are given by different authorities. A discussion of these is out of place here. Such discussions appear in many texts on the diamond and other gems. However, if the bottom facets are inclined 41° and the top facets 35° from the plane of the girdle, excellent brilliancy will result.

Equipment Needed.—Items needed for this work and that have not been called for in previous work are:

A vertical spindle in bearings that will hold it positively true at speeds up to 2200rpm. See Fig. 42.

A Belgian Cast Iron wheel (The diamond worker never calls it a lap).

A device for holding the dop in proper position on the wheel. The professional uses a tong as shown in Fig. 43. The front end of this tong is split and holds the stem of the dop. Several of these tongs are shown grouped around the wheel in Fig. 42.

Figure 42.—DIAMOND POLISHERS WHEEL SHOWING TONGS, DOP, ETC.

Figure 43.—CLOSE-UP OF TONG SHOWING DOP STEM
CLAMPED IN PLACE.

A dop.   A metal cup with a stem of about 1/8″ copper wire
which is clamped in the tong.

Some No. 4 diamond dust.

Some solder.   A mixture of approximately half lead and
half tin that is used for embedding the diamond on the dop.

A saw if desired.   The machine consists of a horizontal
spindle capable of running true at 6000 rpm and with an adjustable arm for feeding the diamond to the saw by gravity.   The
cutting tool is a disc of phosphor bronze from 3″ to 5″ in
diameter and from 3 to 10 thousandths of an inch in thickness.
This is initially charged by rolling diamond dust into its edge.

Operation—Cleaving.—Every diamond crystal has eight
cleavage planes.   The ideal crystal is in the form of two four-
sided pyramids, base to base.   The crystal will split just as a
block of wood splits, parallel to any of these faces.   The cleaver
polishes a small face on the stone to enable him to look with a
microscope within the stone and observe its structure.   This
preliminary study may take hours, but the actual cleaving takes
only a few minutes.   After the cleaver has determined just
where the stone should be split, he mounts the stone in cement
on the end of a stick.   Then with a sharp sliver of diamond
mounted on another stick, he proceeds, by rubbing the sliver
back and forth in one place, to scratch a deep groove on the

surface of the stone at the place where and in the direction that he wishes the stone to split. Then setting the stick upright in a holder, he places a knife blade in the scratch. A sharp light rap with a light hammer on the knife blade splits off a flake with its flat base parallel to a natural face of the octahedron.

Cleaving is not a necessary part of the shaping of every diamond. Cleaving is not done to save time but to save gem material. If the slab that would be removed by cleaving is not of sufficient size and of proper quality to furnish one or more gems, the part is polished away instead of being cleaved off. Cleaving is also used when a large stone has in it a flaw which would injure a single large gem cut from the crystal. The crystal is then cleaved in such a way as to remove the flaw and permit the cutting of two or more perfect gems. The amateur will probably have little use for cleaving.

Operation—Sawing.—Sawing, like cleaving, is used, not to save time but to save gem material. Therefore small crystals are not usually sawed, but the surplus material is polished away. The sawing machine, as has been described under "equipment," consists of a horizontal spindle carrying a disc saw, and an adjustable arm which may be turned into any position to present to the saw any desired face of the crystal. The arm has on it a travel limiting screw which prevents the saw's cutting quite through the crystal in the absence of the operator. The arm feeds the crystal to the saw by gravity. The disc is of phosphor bronze from 3″ to 5″ in dia. and from 3 to 10 thousandths of an inch in thickness. No. 4 diamond dust mixed with olive oil is rolled into its edge. The pressure at the beginning of the cut is very slight, probably a fraction of an ounce, and the cut is usually begun with a thick saw. After the cut is deep enough to insure that the edge of the saw will not jump out of the cut and be ruined by bending, a thinner saw is put on and the pressure increased to probably two or three pounds. The speed of this saw is 6000 rpm. The diamond is held on the arm either by a mechanical holder or by being embedded in a melted solder of approximately half lead and half tin. When the stone is embedded in the solder, no part of it is exposed except that part which is to be sawed off. A clamp is placed on the diamond to hold it firmly in its seat. The saw recharges itself continually with particles ground off the diamond, but it should be frequently lubricated with olive oil. The time required for sawing cannot be predicted. Diamonds vary greatly in hardness, and the condition of the saw is not constant. Ordinarily the sawing of 1/64 sq. in. of diamond (1/8″ square) should require from 2 to 4 hours.

In mounting the crystal in the melted metal, the metal is not allowed to become liquid but only mushy. While in this mushy state it is formed into a pyramid or semi-sphere with a special tool. This is essentially a pair of large tweezers about 11″ long by 1 1/4″ wide. With the aid of this tool the mushy metal is made into a crude pyramid. It is then smoothed off and formed to the correct shape by drawing the tweezers over the top and side of dop, at the same time turning the dop slowly in the wooden block in which it is being supported for this operation. Fig. 44 illustrates the layout. The picture is from an actual operation. Three burners are being heated by gas flames. The one on the left has some lead discs resting on the top of the brass cup. When these become mushy, the worker lifts the cup from the flame and places it in the wooden block. He uses, for doing this, the pair of tongs shown lying on the bench. Then with the large tweezers he forms the lead to a shape similar to the other two dops that are being heated on the other two flames. The bowl at the end of the bench is partly filled with water and is used to cool the dop after the diamond has been set. When the pyramid has been made into proper shape, and while the metal is still soft, the diamond is placed in proper position with a pair of tweezers, and the soft metal is moulded around it. The diamond worker handles the molten metal with his bare fingers in giving the final touches, but this is not a trick to be tried by the beginner. For reasons already

Figure 44.—DOPS BEING HEATED IN GAS FLAME.

noted the amateur will not often have occasion to do sawing, and as the equipment is delicate and must be accurate, and as these characteristics cost money, it is not likely that many amateurs will do any great amount of sawing.

Operation—Cutting or Bruting.—The diamond worker does not speak of the grinding of a gem on the wheel as "cutting." He calls that polishing. "Cutting" is to him the rubbing together of two stones to remove surplus material. Most of the books refer to this as "bruting." When there is definitely a large surplus of material to be removed, and cleaving is not justifiable and sawing would be too costly, it can often be done advantageously by rubbing together two stones, both being cemented to sticks. This is done over a box or a pan to save the cut away material.

Operation—Polishing.—The spindle with its wheel and the tong and the dop have all been described. Also the metal cement and the method of moulding it around a stone.

The stone is first ground to 4 main facets plus the table on the top and to 4 main facets on the bottom. In this eight squaring operation the stone is pressed into the solder to where only one facet is exposed at a time. In cutting the smaller facets several can often be cut with one setting. It was mentioned that the dop is attached to a stem of copper wire about 1/8" dia. and that this wire is held in the tong. The bending of this wire is the only adjustment provided for presenting the gem in proper position to the wheel.

The wheel is made of a fine grained imported Belgian cast iron. It is initially conditioned by machining to an absolutely flat surface. Then a Carborundum or emery block is rubbed radially over all the surface of the wheel. This is called "scouring" and is to score the face to provide seats for the diamond dust. In preparing a new lap about 20 drops of olive oil is mixed with 1 carat of No. 4 diamond dust. A small amount of this is rubbed on the lap. The pressure of the diamond being ground forces the dust into the lap. The ground away diamond from the gem helps to keep the lap charged. Grinding can now proceed. The lap speed should be about 2200 rpm. (With a lap 10" to 12" dia.) This operation is not fast. Polishing a single main facet on a 1 carat gem may take from 20 minutes to several hours. The stone must be so set that polishing is across the grain. If the stone is properly set and the stone is properly lubricated, the dop will not have to be removed for cooling.

Note that this system does not first grind and then polish but that the operation polishes as it grinds.

When a wheel surface becomes rough and scored it must be resurfaced the same as a new lap. The stone should be frequently moved on the wheel to place it in a new path and avoid scoring of the wheel.

It does not pay to try to reclaim diamond dust from polishing wheels.

The photograph Fig. 42 does not entirely make clear how the tong is held in place. A metal "tong plate" is anchored to the wood bench with lag screws. At both front and rear end it has an upright pin. The tong proper rides against the front one of these. A pin projecting from the rear of the tong rides against the rear upright pin. These bearings hold the tong in place against the pull of the wheel.

Lead plates are placed on the tong to give proper pressure to the diamond on the wheel. The amount of pressure is varied by moving the plates toward or away from the wheel.

The only limit to the number of gems that can be cut at one time on one wheel is the number of tongs that can be grouped around the wheel.

Diamonds, like sapphires, have "knots" in them. These are very similar to knots in wood. Sometimes they may be ground flat by perseverance. Sometimes they cannot be ground and the cutting of a gem must be abandoned and the crystal either cleaved to a smaller size or used for some other purpose.

CHAPTER XV

MISCELLANEOUS USEFUL INFORMATION

Mohs Scale of Hardness

1. Talc
2. Gypsum
3. Calcite
4. Fluor
5. Apatite
6. Orthoclase
7. Quartz
8. Topaz
9. Corundum
10. Diamond

Weights

15.43 Troy grains	= 1	gram
31.103 grams	= 1	Troy ounce.
28.35 grams	= 1	avoirdupois ounce
1 Troy ounce	= 155.51	Metric carats.
1 Metric carat	= 1/5 gram.	

Distinction Between Precious and Semi-Precious Stones

There is no fixed line between the two.

All authorities class diamond, emerald, and corundum as precious. Most authorities also class pearls and the finest of opals as precious.

Bauers Edelsteinkunde classes the following as precious stones:

Diamond, Corundum, Chrysoberyl, Spinel, Topaz, Beryl, Euclase, Zircon, Tourmaline, Olivine, Spodumene, Fire Opal, Persian Turquoise.

Measures

1 Millimeter (mm.) = approximately 1/25".
1 Centimeter (cm.) = 10 millimeter.

Table of Characteristics of Gem Materials

NAME	HARDNESS	REFRACTIVE INDEX
Amber	2—2 1/2	1.54
Anatase	5 1/2—6	2.55—2.49
Andalusite	7—7 1/2	1.64
Apatite	5	1.64
Axinite	6 1/2	1.68
Azurite	3 1/2	1.71
Benitoite	6 1/2	1.76—1.80
Beryl	7 1/2—8	1.58
Beryllonite	5 1/2—6	1.56
Cassiterite	6—7	2.04
Chlorastrolite	5—6	
Chromite	5 1/2	
Chrysoberyl	8 1/2	1.75
Chrysocolla	2—4	1.50
Cobaltite	5 1/2	
Coral	3 1/2	
Corundum	9	1.76
Cyanite	4—7	1.72
Datolite	5—5 1/2	1.65
Diamond	10	2.42
Diopside	5—6	1.68
Enstatite	5—6	1.67—1.70
Epidote	6—7	1.75
Euclase	7 1/2	1.65
Feldspar	6—6 1/2	1.52—1.58
Fluorite	4	1.434
Garnet:		
Grossularite	6 1/2—7 1/2	1.735
Pyrope	ditto	1.705
Almandite	ditto	1.83
Rhodolite	ditto	
Andradite	ditto	1.895
Gypsum	2	1.525
Hematite	5 1/2—6 1/2	
Iolite	7—7 1/2	1.55
Jade:		
Jadeite	6 1/2—7	1.66
Nephrite	ditto	1.62
Jet	2—2 1/2	
Lazulite	5—6	1.62
Lazurite	5—5 1/2	1.50

Malachite	3 1/2	1.81
Moldavite	5 1/2	1.50—1.60
Obsidian	5 1/2	1.50—1.60
Olivine	6 1/2—7	1.68
Opal	5 1/2—6 1/2	1.44—1.45
Pearl	2 1/2—3 1/2	
Phenacite	7 1/2—8	1.66
Prehnite	6—7	1.63
Pyrite	6—6 1/2	
Quartz	7	1.55
Rhodonite	5—6	1.73
Rutile	6—6 1/2	2.62—2.90
Sepiolite	2—2 1/2	1.55
Smithsonite	5	1.75
Sodalite	5—6	1.48
Spinel	8	1.72
Spodumene	6—7	1.66
Staurolite	7—7 1/2	1.74
Thomsonite	5—5 1/2	1.51
Titanite	5—5 1/2	1.90—2.03
Topaz	8	1.62—1.63
Tourmaline	7—7 1/2	1.63
Turquoise	6	1.63
Variscite	4—5	
Vesuvianite	6 1/2	1.72
Willemite	5—6	1.70
Zircon	7 1/2	1.92—1.95
Zoisite:		
Thulite	6—6 1/2	1.70

*Where two figures are given in the Refractive Index column, it has not been stated if the two represent the values of the ordinary and the extraordinary rays, or a variation in the mean index. To the cutter, in actual practice this is not important, as he works no closer than to place a particular material in a special group such as "topaz, R. I. 1.65." If exact information is needed for technical purposes, it should be gotten from a text on Mineralogy.

Comparative Hardness of some Common Gems

Quartz = 1
Topaz = 2
Corundum = 12
Diamond = 1000

CHAPTER XVI

SOURCES OF SUPPLY FOR EQUIPMENT AND MATERIAL

It is a rather hazardous business to attempt to give, in a work of this kind, definite sources of supply. Naturally there are many sources of supply for many of the items. Naturally also, when only one or only a few sources are mentioned, others with products equally meritorious must be neglected. Also, this text may be referred to many years from now, when sources of supply will have changed. Yet some attempt at listing must be made, as lack of this information is a terrific handicap to the beginner.

It is preferable that buyers of materials get and read the magazines, Rocks and Minerals, Peekskill, N. Y., and The Mineralogist, 409 Couch Bldg., Portland, Ore. In their pages will be found many advertisements of gem materials. For the convenience of the reader the following list is given of suppliers of gem materials. These suppliers are in general advertisers in the pages of the magazines mentioned and are listed merely as such:

Ward's National Science Establishment, Rochester, N. Y.—General.

John A. Renshaw, 1038 Baldwin Ave., Arcadia, Calif.—Opals.

John M. Greiger, 405 Ninita Parkway, Pasadena, Calif.—General.

Franklin G. McIntosh, 841 Greenway Drive, Beverley Hills, Calif.—General.

Angus & Coote, 500 George St., Sydney, Australia—Opals.

Smith Agate Shop, 228 S. W. Alder St., Portland, Ore.—Agates, etc.

John A. Grenzig, 299 Adams St., Brooklyn, N. Y.—General.

Enos F. Heyward, 1927 Portland Ave., St. Paul, Minn.—General.

Scott Rose Quartz Co., Custer, S. Dak.—Rose Quartz.

L. W. Stillwell Curio Store, Deadwood, S. Dak.—General.

E. A. Southwick, 528 S. E. Washington St., Portland, Ore.—Agates, etc.

Greene's Agate Shop, 757 E. Revere St., Bend, Ore.—General.

J. Lewis Renton, 3366 N. E. Beeky St., Portland, Ore.—Agates, etc.

Charles Simpson, Quincy, Washington—Agate, etc.

So. Oregon Mineral Exchange, 620 S. Ivy St., Medford, Ore.—Agate, etc.

Georg O. Wild, Idar, Germany—General.

R. W. Tuthill, 110 Earl Road, Michigan City, Ind.—General.

N. H. Seward, 457 Bourke St., Melbourne, Australia—Opals.

W. E. Troupe, Jordan Station, Ontario, Can.—Sodalite.

The Gem Shop, Box 15A, Helena, Mont.—General.

R. H. Van Esselstyne, 3 Maiden Lane, New York, N. Y.—Emeralds.

Albert Everitt, Escondido, Calif.—General.

Frank Duncan, Terlingula, Tex.—Agate, etc.

P. L. Forbes, Stauffer, Ore.—Obsidian, agate, etc.

L. E. Bowser, Bairoil, Wyo.—Moss Agates.

Peerless Gem Shop, Box 72, Penryn, Calif.—Agates, etc.

Mosaic Studios, Joseph City, Ariz. Agatized wood, etc.

Ruddimann's Agate Shop, Newport, Ore.—Agates, etc.

Anthony Espositer, 64 W. 48th St., New York, N. Y.—Fine Gems.

Stephen Varni, 11 Maiden Lane, New York, N. Y.—Fine Gems and rough gem materials.

Suppliers of equipment are not so numerous, and fortunately some few of these suppliers can furnish practically anything needed for gem cutting. Following list covers suppliers from whom all needed items can be gotten:

Wm. Dixon, Inc., Box 593, Newark, N. J.—General.

Waldru Lapidary Shop, 2267 N. Dearborn St., Indianapolis, Ind.—General.

The Carborundum Co., Niagara Falls, N. Y., Abrasive wheels and powders.

The Norton Co., Worchester, Mass.—Abrasive wheels and powders.

The Prang Co., 36 W. 24th St., New York, N. Y.—Clay Flour.

As a convenience to the novice collecting his equipment, we list the chief items he will need, together with their source of supply. The failure to mention any prices is deliberate. It can only be said that at the present time the total cost of equipment for cabochon cutting should be about $50.00. That the equipment for diamond sawing should cost from $5.00 to $10.00. That the equipment for facet cutting will cost about $50.00. And that the equipment for engraving may cost anything from $25.00 to several hundred dollars, depending on its elaborateness and also on its quality. All such figures are necessarily subject to great variation. Many men are equipped to make much of their equipment. Others show great ingenuity in adapting to the job in hand such equipment as they may have on hand or that they can buy cheap or that they can salvage from junk yards. Others wish to do as little as possible of their making and assembling. So figures given above must not be taken too literally, as so many elements are involved.

The amateur usually begins with the cutting of cabochons. For this work he will need:

1 workbench_____Make locally
1 1/4 H. P. 1800 rpm motor_____Wm. Dixon, Inc.
1 Bench grinder with 3/4" shaft_____Wm. Dixon, Inc.

1 8" x 1" No. 100-J-G5 Carborundum wheel
1 8" x 1" No. FF-K-G4 Carborundum wheel
5 lbs. No. 100 Carborundum grains
5 lbs. No. FF Carborundum grains

> Wm. Dixon, or Carborundum Co., or Norton Co.

1 6" x 3/4" cast iron lap_____Wm. Dixon
1 2" x 8" wood lap with true periphery_____ " "
2 1" x 6" Rock hard felt wheels_____ " "
5 lbs. Medium pumice powder_____ " "
1 Lb. Tin oxide_____ " "
2 lbs. Hard chasers cement_____ " "
1 7 power to 10 power magnifying glass_____ " "
Sufficient splash pans (See text)_____Make or buy locally
Sufficient reservoirs (See text)_____Make or buy locally
Lap sticks_____Make locally
Oil cloth apron_____Buy locally
Sponges for water feed_____Buy locally
Several 1" paint brushes_____Buy locally
1 Wheel dresser_____Wm. Dixon, Inc.

The equipment for sawing depends of course on the method used. If the "mud saw" is used, there will be required:

1 Stone holding device_____Make locally

5 lbs No. 100 Carborundum grains_____

> Wm. Dixon, Inc. or Carborundum Co., or Norton Co.

1 Sawing reservoir__J. A. Piper Roofing Co., Greenville, S. C.
Several sheet metal discs_____Buy locally

If the diamond saw is to be used, there will be needed:

1 Stone holding device_____Make locally
1 reservoir_____Have made locally
1 Diamond saw—See advertisements in magazines referred to above.

Those wishing to make their own diamond saw can get:
Copper discs—Oregon Sheet Metal Works, 618 S. W. Front St., Portland, Ore.
Smith's Agate Shop, 228 S. W. Alder St., Portland, Ore.
Diamond dust—Arthur A. Crafts Co., 161 Brookline Ave.—Boston, Mass.

Diamond drills can be gotten. from Arthur A. Crafts Co., 161 Brookline Ave., Boston, Mass.

Bead rounding mills should be made in local foundry and machine shops.
Face plate type of lap should be made in local foundry and machine shops.
Low priced drill presses may be gotten from Wm. Dixon, Inc. or from national mail order houses.

The equipment for faceting can all be gotten from Wm. Dixon and consists of:

1 faceting device (for holding gem)
1 6" x 3/4" cast iron lap
1 6" x 3/4" tin lap
1 lb. gem cutters hard cement

For carving soft stone the tools had best be made at home or by a local blacksmith. In this way the cost is slight. The steel for these tools and the handles for them can be gotten from Wm. Dixon, Inc. The camera lucida can be gotten from various novelty supply houses. The riffle files can be gotten from Wm. Dixon, Inc.

The engraving and carving outfit for hard gems may cost whatever one wishes to put into it. The cost of the lathe itself may vary greatly, depending on how rugged it is and how true it is made. The chief cost of such an outfit is in the points used. The beginner should have made only a few simple points at first and add to the supply as he determines from experience what shapes will prove most valuable to him. It is the Author's opinion that all this equipment had best be made in local shops. And certainly the work should be done by a good machinist. There is nothing more annoying than such an outfit having lost motion or with points that are not true.

The carving of soft stones with revolving tools and Carborundum points is another job in which the worker should begin with small equipment and add to it. The points can be gotten from Wm. Dixon, Inc. or from the Carborundum Co.

Amber colored transparent bakelite and bakelite resin can be gotten from The Bakelite Corporation, 247 Park Ave., New York, N. Y.

Good work in gem mounting is done at reasonable prices by:
Smith's Agate Shop, 228 S. W. Alder St., Portland, Ore.
Ray F. Parker, 248 S. W. Morrison St., Portland, Ore.

Carborundum Buffing Powder can be gotten from The Carborundum Co. or from Wm. Dixon, Inc.

Alumina (for polishing) and Norbide (for cutting) can be gotten from either The Norton Co. or Wm. Dixon, Inc.

CPSIA information can be obtained
at www.ICGtesting.com
Printed in the USA
BVOW04s1022291016

466056BV00002B/65/P